Give Me
AN OLD SHOE

☙

Gene Schuyler

Give Me An Old Shoe

Copyright © 2013 by Gene Schuyler

First Printing 2013

All rights reserved. No part of this publication may be reproduced, stored in a

Retrieval system or transmitted in any form by any means, electronic,

Mechanical, photocopy, recording or otherwise without prior permission of the publisher, except as provided by USA copyright law.

ISBN: 978-0-615-15131-1

Scripture quotations are from the King James Version of the Bible unless otherwise stated.

Printed in the United States of America

Cover photo: Marie Schuyler

ଊ INTRODUCTION ଈ

It all began as a little boy back in my home town of Florence, South Carolina, the very first day on a baseball field for the first time at the age of five and hearing my name called as a member of a team. I will never forget the thrill of wearing that baseball uniform with the name of "Whistle," an orange drink bottling company, on the front and the number 12 on the back. I was the smallest, of course, on the team, yet with a big heart and desire to be a "ball player" in the big leagues, was all that was on my mind. I knew that I had to prove myself to be a regular member of the team, so I worked hard every day to improve my skills.

I remember that to improve my fielding, I would take a golf ball, throw it against the wall of the schoolhouse and work on my skills as a fielder. I would throw up rocks in the air and hit them with a bat to improve my swing; yes, I destroyed many a bat and golf ball, needless to say many bruises, but it was worth it.

Years went by and I continued to improve and grow; all I knew and thought of was baseball, baseball, and more baseball. Time moved on fast and I grew up and I wanted to be the best and play on the best of the teams. I grew up on the east side of town and we didn't get the best of equipment and playing fields that was on the other side of town and we rarely played the teams from "over there."

The thrill of the next three years of growing and experiencing being "a hero" was unexpected of me, since I was small in stature. Let me explain it this way. It was a big ball game for us as we were playing one of the teams from "across town" on our field. Somehow that day, it came together for me. The newspaper read the next day, **"Turley/Schuyler star in victory."** Turley was our pitcher and pitched a beautiful game and I went 3 for 4 and one of them being my first homerun. What a thrill for an eight year old, his name in the local newspaper headlines!

As I got older, and improved in my playing abilities, I wanted to play on the other side of town teams, but not living over there, how could I? Then it came to me that if I pretended to live over there, I could get a chance. Well, one day, I started by riding the city bus to the ball field on the other side of town, and hoping for a chance to play.

When I finally arrived I was wowed by the green outfield, the fence, for on my side of town, there was no real green outfield, no fence and no dugouts, for you that are not familiar with this term, a place for the guys to sit, under a roof out of the sun. My heart pounded so loud that I could feel it pushing out my shirt.

Well, the time came to sign up, which I did, and was put on a team and given this beautiful uniform, one that fit, and I began a new life on a new team on a new field.

Time went by and even though I wasn't the best, nor did I make the first nine players, I got to be a substitute, well I wasn't all that excited about that, but it was better than back on my side of town, where the ball field was nowhere close to what I was now playing on. I learned then, without knowing it, that in life everyone cannot be number one, there has to be a number two.

As I grew older, and playing for different teams, I came to realize that no matter how good I was, there was one better than me and that I was expendable, if necessary, to win a game. For instance, I remember during a "pony league" game, I guess I was around fourteen, that we were not winning and I was playing when one of our best players broke his spikes and my coach, rather than taking him out and replacing him, he pulled me and *gave him my shoes*, since we wore the same size shoe, and pulled me out of the game and replaced me with a player that was not as *"good"* as me and kept in the "special" guy. Needless to say, I was very dejected; yes, we won, but I finally realized that I would never be a number one and that I was to be willing to be a substitute, if necessary, for the team and this was the beginning without me realizing it. That is what life is all about and without knowing that in my future, as a preacher of the word of God and a pastor, time would come for me to learn that it is not important to be number one, but a servant to man and most of all to my Lord.

I am now seventy three and have been in the ministry for over forty four years and have had the privilege and honor to serve my Lord in so many ways. I have been pastor of five churches and a staff member of the one I now presently serve as membership pastor.

Sometimes it is hard to be a follower in leadership when you have been the "number one man." Then I remember what a dear friend, Curtis Hutson, who is now in heaven, said to me when I felt that my peers did not understand my early ministry not growing as quickly as they thought we should have, and even that maybe God did not send me to the area I was pastor, *"Many times when God needs to drive a nail and can't find a hammer, He leans down and picks up an old shoe to get the job done."* This is my prayer and desire for my life in my latter years to be what God wants and where He wants me to be. We all can't be the number one, **by the way, God is to be number ONE,** but you and I can be a shoe that He can use for His Glory and in the reaching and teaching the lost and helping the saved grow in as many ways as necessary.

So with this all said, this is a book about what it really means to be a servant of our Lord Jesus Christ and to follow his leadership in this area of our lives if we are going to reach the lost and unchurched, and then to be the disciples that we need to be in helping others to grow in God's Word.

> ## *"gave Him my shoes"*

What have you ever given up to serve someone and why?

_____
_____
_____
_____
_____
_____

What was it and what were the results and would you do it again?

_____
_____
_____
_____
_____
_____

ACKNOWLEDGEMENTS

To Evangelist Junior Hill for his much encouragement and support through the years and being a "real" friend and prayer warrior, servant and Bible expositor and his encouragement for me to continue writing.

I want to thank the members of Mid-Way Baptist Church of Raleigh, North Carolina, for allowing me to serve with them for many years.

To my wife, Marie, whom I believe is one of the greatest servants I know, and for her tireless energy in serving her Savior in all the churches we have served, without complaint.

To Dr. James Dees, pastor and friend for his kind words for my first book and his support through the years.

It was Billy Graham that said, *"Be honest about your weakness and ask God to help you overcome them so you can serve Christ more effectively.*

"GIVE ME AN OLD SHOE"

☙ *Give Me An Old Shoe* ❧

Table of Contents

Introduction v
Acknowledgements ix
Let's Get Started xii

Chapter 1   Servanthood - "OUR EXAMPLE" 13

Chapter 2   Servanthood - "RELATIONSHIPS" 25

Chapter 3   Servanthood - "THE HEART" 36

Chapter 4   Servanthood - "WHO WE ARE" 53

Chapter 5   Servanthood - "THE DESIRE ~ HOW TO SERVE" 63

Chapter 6   Servanthood - "THE ABILITY TO SERVE" 72

Chapter 7   Servanthood - "BEING A GIVER" 85

Chapter 8   Servanthood - "LIVING IT OUT" 107

Chapter 9   Servanthood - "THE SECRET OF SERVING" 120

Chapter 10   Servanthood - "THE COST" 132

Chapter 11   Servanthood - "THY WILL LORD" 147

॰ Let's Get Started ॰

With all the Bible teaching down through the years in strong Bible Believing churches, I find that the ministry that our Savior taught us on being a servant has greatly diminished.

We are living in a society that is self-centered and wants everyone to do for them. This book is about finding out what God expects of every born again believer and that being a servant is not a "weighty matter" but one of following our Lord's example and that it is more blessed to give than receive.

How to get the most out of this book?

As we go through this book you will find how and why Jesus taught us to become followers of Him in this area of serving Him and others.

We will follow our Savior's example and other Bible characters of what it means to be a servant and the joy of knowing that we have done what our Master has taught us.

As we study this book, we will find the "True meaning of servanthood," what the Biblical concept of servant hood is all about and what servanthood requires of each of us.

It is my goal of this book and series to understand, as a Christian, how important it is to serve our Savior and our fellow man.

All through and sometimes at the end of each chapter you will find questions that pertain to the chapter to help you think through that which you have just studied and how it will affect your life as a servant.

∞ 1 ∞

~ Servanthood ~

"OUR EXAMPLE"

"Let this mind be in you which was also in Christ Jesus"

(Philippians 2:5).

It is Jesus Christ, the beloved Redeemer of our souls, who speaks thus. He had just humbled Himself to do the work of the slave and washed His disciples' feet. In doing so, His love had rendered to the body the service of which it stood in need at the supper table. At the same time He had shown, in a striking symbol, what He had done for their souls in cleansing them from sin. In this twofold work of love, He had thus set before them, just before parting, in one significant act, the whole work of His life as a ministry of blessing to body and to soul and as He sits down He says: ***"I have given you an example, that ye also should do, even as I have done to you"*** *(John 13:15).* All that they had seen in Him, and experienced from Him, is thus made the rule of their life: The word of the blessed Savior is for us too. To each one who knows that the Lord has washed away his sins, the command comes with all the touching force of one of the last words of Him who was going out to die for us.

CHAPTER ONE

Jesus Christ does indeed ask every one of us in everything to act just as we have seen Him do. What He has done to ourselves, and still does each day, we are to do over again to others. In His condescending, pardoning, saving love, He is our example; each of us is to be the copy and image of the Master.

The thought comes at once: "how little have I lived thus; how little have I even known that I was expected thus to live! And yet, He is my lord; He loves me, and I love Him; I dare not entertain the thought of living otherwise than He would have me live." What can I do but open my heart to His word, and fix my gaze on His example, until it builds its divine power upon me, and draws me with irresistible force to cry: ***"Lord, even as Thou hast done, so will I do also."*** The power of an example depends chiefly on two things.

1. The one is the attractiveness of what it gives us to see.

2. The personal relation and influence of Him in whom it is seen.

In both aspects, what power there is in our Lord's example! Or, is there really anything very attractive in our Lord's example? We must all ask it in earnest, because, if there was ever a time in our world today it is that the Spirit of God would open our eyes to see the heavenly beauty of the likeness of the only-begotten Son!

We know who the Lord Jesus is. He is the Son of the all-glorious God, one with the Father in nature and glory and perfection. When He had been on earth it could be said of Him, "We show you that eternal life which was with the Father, and was manifested unto us." In Him, we see God. In Him, we see how God would act when He was here in our place on earth. In Him, all that is beautiful and lovely and perfect in the heavenly world is revealed to us in the form of an earthly life. If we want to see what is really exciting and wonderful in the heavenly world, if we would see what is really divine, we have only to look at Jesus; in all He does, the glory of God is shown forth.

But, oh how sad the blindness of God's children today in this self-centered society. This heavenly beauty has to many of them no attraction; there is no form or comeliness that they should desire it for it is, *"what is in it for me?"*

I like what Andrew Murray said, *"The manners and the way of living, in the court of an earthly king exercise influence throughout the empire. The example it gives is imitated by all who belong to the nobility or the higher classes. But the examples of the King of heaven, who came and dwelt in the flesh, that we might see how we might here on earth live a God-like life."* As I watch the flow of the present day church, I wonder how few of Christ's followers it does really find imitating. When we at the example of Jesus and His obedience to the will of His Father, see His humiliation to be a servant of the most unworthy we find His love as shown in the entire giving up and sacrifice of Himself, and we see the most wondrous and glorious example heaven has to show; in heaven itself we shall see nothing greater or brighter.

With such an example, given to us by God on every purpose to make the imitation attractive and possible, it should encourage and give us a desire to be like Christ. Is it not enough to stir all that is within us with a holy jealousy and with joy unutterable as we hear the message, "I have given you an example, that even as I have done, ye should also do?"

Jesus had not washed the feet of others in the presence of His disciples; it was when He had washed *their feet* that He said: "Even as I have done *to you*, ye should also do." It is the consciousness of a personal relationship to Christ that enforces the command: "Do as I have done." It is the experience of what Jesus has done to you and me that is the strength in which we can go and do the same to others. He never asks that we do more than has been done

CHAPTER ONE

to us. But not less either: EVEN AS I have done to you. He does not ask that I shall humble myself as a servant deeper than He has done.

Christ only demands that we shall just do and be what He, the King, has done and been. He humbled Himself, as low as humiliation could go, to love and to bless us. He counted this ***His highest honor and blessedness***. And now, what a privilege; He invites us to partake of the same honor and blessedness, in loving and serving others as He did. The heavenly loveliness of the great Example, and the Divine lovingness of the great Example, combines to make the Example above everything attractive. Truly, if I indeed know the love that rests on me, and the humiliation through which alone that love could reach me, and the power of the cleansing which has washed me, nothing can keep me back from saying "only to be like you Lord." Only there is one thing I must not forget. It is not the remembrance of what Jesus has once done to me, but the living experience of what He is now to me, that will give me the power to act like Him. His love must be a present reality, the inflowing of a life and a power in which I can love like Him. It is only by the Holy Spirit, I realize what Jesus is doing for me, and how He does it, and that it is HE who does it, that it is possible for me to do for others what He is doing for me.

My question to you dear reader is, "shall not our whole heart joyously respond to His command?"

Jesus is our servant/leader and in His ministry on earth, He taught us the meaning of servanthood and leadership. He was essentially a leader and undoubtedly a servant. In His personality, He displayed both characteristics. He was a servant, and He was a leader, so then we are called to be servant/leaders as we found in the above text.

"I have given you an example that *ye also* should do *even* as I have done to you" (John 13:15 NKJV).

GIVE ME AN OLD SHOE

The Greek word "doulos" is translated in the New Testament both as "bond slave" and as "servant." The words have a similar meaning. Jesus came as a servant, as a slave. He was the servant of the Lord, just as all Christians are called to be servants of the servant of the Lord.

Up to now, what stands out about Christ as your example?

_____
_____
_____
_____
_____
_____

Let's now see in what ways Jesus was the leader of servanthood.

1. In Jesus Christ we see the marks of a true LEADER.

Jesus was a born leader for we find this that at age 12 when He was showing indications of future leadership as He conversed with the wisest minds among the religious leaders in Jerusalem (Luke 2:47).

Then, during His three year ministry, Jesus was the leader. He had all the marks of leadership. He attracted people to Him. They left their nets, the tax collector's table, their revolutionary political activity, their other tasks, and followed Him. Jesus was the leader.

Follow with me now as we look at the marks of Jesus:

a) Jesus was a leader because of His divine nature:

John the Baptist declared, at the River Jordan, that one was in their midst, the sandals on whose feet John was unworthy to tie.

CHAPTER ONE

The voice of the Father was heard at Jesus' baptism, "Thou art my beloved Son; in thee I am well pleased" (Luke 3:22). Jesus, the one who declared Himself, "the way, the truth and the life" (John 14:6), who answered that "I and my Father are one" (John 10:30).

b) Jesus was a leader by His example:

Jesus set the standard by which all leadership is to be assessed. He was the natural leader. He did not have to raise His voice to be heard. When He entered the room, a hush fell over the people. He was a born leader. He sets for us an example of strong, sensitive leadership for all who presume to a leadership position.

c) Jesus was a leader by His action:

When action was needed, Jesus acted. Jesus had opened His ministry with a similar act, (John 2:13-25). Now, three years later, the temple was defiled again by the "religious business" of the leaders. They had turned the court of the Gentiles into a place where foreign Jews could exchange money and purchase sacrifices. What had begun as a service and convenience for visitors from other lands soon turned into a lucrative business.

But the presence of this "religious market" turned many sensitive Gentiles away from the witness of Israel. The court of the Gentiles was used for mercenary business, not missionary business.

When Jesus called the temple "My house," He was affirming that He is God. When He called it "My house of prayer,"

He was quoting Isaiah 56:7. The entire 56th chapter of Isaiah denounces the unfaithful leaders of Israel. The phrase "den of robbers" comes from Jeremiah 7:11 and is part of a long sermon that Jeremiah delivered in the gate of the temple, rebuking the people for the same sins that Jesus saw and judged in His day.

Jesus was a strong man, a decisive leader. He confronted what was wrong or harmful and led by action.

d) Jesus was a leader by the example of His life:

Jesus grew in favor with God and with men and women (Luke 2:52). He went around doing good (Acts 10:38). The common people heard Him gladly. He spoke with authority, not like the Scribes and the Pharisees (Matthew 7:29).

The apostle Paul often wrote about the "grace of our Lord Jesus Christ" (2 Corinthians 8:9). Jesus was loved by-and loved and prayed for-his friends (John 17). He was such an attractive person that people were drawn to Him like iron filings to a magnet (Luke 4:15).

e) Jesus was a leader by His deep compassion:

Jesus wept over the city of Jerusalem (Luke 13:34). When his friend Lazarus was declared dead, the Scriptures tell us that his strong leader, Jesus, wept for His friend (John 11:35). When the sister of Lazarus was under pressure from her activist sister, Martha, Jesus came to her defense (Luke 10:42). Leadership without compassion is arid and sterile.

f) Jesus was a leader by making the ultimate sacrifice:

Only a person of immense strength could look death squarely in the face and walk unafraid towards it. Only a person of absolute conviction could have endured the whip, and the nails, the thorn, the spear and accepted the loneliness and agony of the Cross.

2. In Jesus we see the marks of a true SERVANT.

There are many New Testament titles for Jesus Christ, but if He preferred only one, I believe that it may have been *"Servant of the Lord."*

a) He offered us a powerful model of servanthood.

b) When not one of His disciples was prepared to wash the accumulated dust off the feet of the disciples (even of Jesus), it was Jesus, the Lord of glory, who took up the basin and towel and washed the feet of his friends (John 13:5).

c) He understood the blessing that accompanies meekness. In Matthew 5, when Jesus taught from a mountain, he set down for posterity the demeanor of the servant.

d) He taught us the obligation of servanthood (Matthew chapter 5).

e) He taught us how to exhibit humility.

f) With this all in mind, it is so important that as Christians, we accept the opportunities of LEADERSHIP that the Lord and His people ask us to do, realizing that we need to be guided by the Holy Spirit to lead us with the spirit of the servant and in so doing we will walk in the steps of Jesus the Christ, the MASTER SERVANT!

CHAPTER ONE

LET'S REVIEW:

1. At what age was Jesus when He taught in the Synagogue?
   _____

2. What was the response of his mother?
   _____

3. Who were the disciples that left their fishing nets?
   _____

4. Who was the tax collector?
   _____

5. What is meant by "Jesus was a leader because of His divine nature?"_____

6. How did Jesus set the example for us to presume leadership position?
   _____

7. When Jesus entered the Temple, in John chapter 2, as a decisive leader, what did He confront and how would you handle such today?
   _____
   _____

8. In what ways can you as servant show compassion? _____
   _____
   _____
   _____

9. Briefly review Matthew chapter 5 and how Jesus taught us the obligation of servanthood.

_____
_____
_____

๏ 2 ๛

~ Servanthood ~

"RELATIONSHIPS"

GIVE ME AN OLD SHOE

൲

*S*erving others certainly can be tough; we do so by expending our energies and resources in the interest of others. I believe this is best demonstrated by our Lord on the night prior to His going to the cross. There in the upper room with His disciples, He did the unthinkable; He washed their feet, and The Master became the servant and took the towel. The greatest and highest became the least and the lowest. Christ was able to do this because He was secure in Himself. He knew who He was and where he was going, but He also served His disciples because He loved them. While these two reasons would be adequate in and of themselves, our Lord had another reason for His actions. If you notice that when He had finished washing the disciples' feet, He told them, "I have given you an example, that you should do as I have done to you." (John 13:15). Jesus didn't tell them to do "what" He had done; He commanded them to do "as" He had done. You see, Jesus was teaching them "not" to become full-time foot-washers, but rather full-time servants. If we are going to reach

CHAPTER TWO

the unsaved, there needs to be a full time surrender to service to others.

This brings us another question. Why is it so hard to be a servant? Well let's follow the Lord's example. Read Isaiah 52:13-53:12. Did you get the message?

Good, now place here some personal notes:

_____
_____
_____
_____
_____
_____
_____

As you know as you study history, it was common-place for people to offer sacrifices to the gods, but the notion that a god would make a sacrifice for humans was beyond imagination. The Jewish people themselves had no such concept despite the fact that their own Scriptures predicted it. This is the reason that Jesus after His resurrection said, in Luke 24:25-26, "Then He said to them, O foolish ones, and slow of heart to believe in all that the prophets have spoken! Ought Not the Christ to have suffered these things and to enter into His glory?" (NKJV).

What the disciples overlooked was they overlooked the prophecies about the Suffering Servant who would deliver them from the greater bondage of sin and guilt.

As the Suffering Servant of Isaiah, Jesus clearly communicated His purpose for coming to this earth. Pause now for a moment and turn to the book of Mark chapter 10 and let's look verse 45. "For even the Son of Man did not come to be served, but to serve, and to give His life a ransom for many" (NKJV). Here we find that in His sacrifice on the cross, Jesus provides for us the ultimate illustration of being a servant. All thru the life of Jesus, we see His example of servanthood. He didn't merely talk about being a servant, He lived it out.

In fact, the only reason that He came to this earth was to serve God and through His death and resurrection, to serve humanity. As for His disciples, they became better people in every way after He had met them, than they were before.

This example of servanthood transcends any that has ever been seen, before or since. Just listen to Romans 5:6-8, "For when we were yet without strength, in due time Christ died for the ungodly. For scarcely for a righteous man will one die: yet peradventure for a good man some would even dare to die. But God commendeth his love toward us, in that, while we were yet sinners, Christ died for us."

So in fact, Christ "took up our infirmities and sins and carried our sorrows." If we really believe this, what is it that prevents we that are saved from serving others as He has served us? Now, the Bible also calls on us to be servants.

ALL CHRISTIANS ARE CALLED ON TO BE SERVANTS.

Jesus calls on us to empty ourselves in order to be a child of God. In Matthew 18:2-4, *"And Jesus called a little child unto him, and set him in the midst of them, and said, Verily I say unto you, Except ye be converted, and become as little children, ye shall not enter*

CHAPTER TWO

into the kingdom of heaven. Whosoever therefore shall humble himself as this little child, the same is greatest in the kingdom of heaven."

It is obvious that while we continue with a carnal mind-set we can never become servants of God.

In Romans 8:5-8 we find out **what it means** to be a servant?

1. It is to humble oneself and put the good of others before self.

2. It is to lose your life in service for God and others.

3. It is the opposite of pride and arrogance, or wanting to elevate self.

In John 13:3-17 we see where Jesus defined what it means to be a servant by having:

The Attitude of a servant...

1. is a mindset we adopt - 1 Corinthians 9:19

2. is without consideration of repayment - Luke 6:34-35

3. is unselfish - Philippians 2:3-8

4. is preferential to another, putting others first - Romans 12:10

OUR RELATIONSHIP WITH ONE ANOTHER AND OUR GOD IS TO BE MARKED BY OUR SERVANTHOOD.

We are told that: **We *are to copy our Lord's attitude of service.*** Philippians 2:3-8 and Hebrews 5:8-9.

We are also told that: The *pathway to true greatness is found in service.*

Matthew 23:8-12 *"But you, do not be called 'Rabbi'; for One is your Teacher, the Christ, and you are all brethren. Do not call anyone on earth your father; for One is your Father, He who is in heaven. And do not be called teachers; for One is your Teacher, the Christ. But he who is greatest among you shall be your servant. And whoever exalts himself will be humbled, and he who humbles himself will be exalted" (NKJV).*

WE ARE TO APPLY THE SERVANTHOOD PRINCIPLE TO OUR RELATIONSHIPS IN THE CHURCH.

See what the Scriptures teach us in this area:

Toward one another.

Romans 12:10 – "Be kindly affectionate to one another with brotherly love, in honor giving preference to one another;" (NKJV).

Ephesians 5:21 - "submitting to one another in the fear of God." (NKJV).

Philippians 2:3 - "Let nothing be done through selfish ambition or conceit, but in lowliness of mind let each esteem others better than himself." (NKJV).

CHAPTER TWO

Toward brethren in need.

1 John 3:17 - "But whoever has this world's goods, and sees his brother in need, and shuts up his heart from him, how does the love of God abide in him?" (NKJV).

Toward brethren who are spiritually sick.

Galatians 6:1 - "Brethren, if a man is overtaken in any trespass, you who are spiritual restore such a one in a spirit of gentleness, considering yourself lest you also be tempted" (KNJV).

James 5:19-20 - "Brethren, if anyone among you wanders from the truth, and someone turns him back, let him know that he who turns a sinner from the error of his way will save a soul from death and cover a multitude of sins"(NKJV).

APPLYING THE SERVANTHOOD PRINCIPLE TO EVANGELISM.

If we have the attitude of service we will have compassion on the lost and desire to take the gospel to them.

Jude 22-23 – "And on some have compassion, making a distinction; but others save with fear, pulling them out of the fire, hating even the garment defiled by the flesh" (NKJV).

If we are applying the servant principle we will not be concerned about who "gets credit" for teaching others!

The important thing will be the soul.

If we are applying the servant principle we will not chaff at having to do work, no matter what it is, in the work of saving souls.

GIVE ME AN OLD SHOE

We will want to do whatever it takes to reach out to the Lost.

If we are applying the servant principle, we will not seek converts to "our philosophy" or "our church" but to Christ.

The legend is told of a desert wanderer who found a crystal spring of unsurpassed freshness. The water was so pure he decided to bring some to his king. Barely satisfying his own thirst, he filled a leather bottle with the clear liquid and carried it many days beneath the desert sun before he reached the palace.

When he finally laid his offering at the feet of his sovereign, the water had become stale and rank due to the old container in which it had been stored. But the king would not let his faithful subject even imagine that it was unfit for use. He tasted it with expressions of gratitude and delight, and sent away the loyal heart filled with gladness. After he had gone, others sampled it and expressed their surprise that the king had even pretended to enjoy it. "Ah!" said he, "it was not the water he tasted, but the love that prompted the offering." Many times our service is marked by multiplied imperfections, but the Master looks at our motives and says "It is good."

Final thoughts:

It is important to understand that servanthood relationship is essential to spiritual growth. Friend, if you are not serving God in some way, you are not maturing spiritually (Hebrews 6:10). It is also the purpose for our spiritual gifts and it is also how God carries out His work, (John 14:11-14); and most of all God's work is for every believer!

Today everyone wants to be recognized, but isn't it more exciting to be recognized as a servant, willing to meet the needs of others. Remember, it is our calling is to serve.

CHAPTER TWO

> ☙
> *If we have the attitude of service,*
> *we will have compassion*
> *on the lost and desire*
> *to take the gospel to them.*
> ❧

LET'S REVIEW:

Explain what it means to be a servant based on Romans 8:5-8.

_____
_____
_____
_____
_____
_____
_____
_____
_____
_____
_____
_____

Explain what it means when we say, "The attitude of a servant is a mindset we adopt."

_____
_____
_____
_____
_____

CHAPTER TWO

What do we mean when we say, "we are to copy our Lord's attitude of service"?

_____
_____
_____
_____

Where are you now serving and what are is your spiritual gift(s)?

_____
_____
_____
_____
_____
_____
_____

Personal thoughts:

_____
_____
_____
_____

ꙮ 3 ꙮ

~ Servanthood ~
"THE HEART"

CHAPTER THREE

One of the major problems with Christians today is readily seen in slogans like, "be all you can be" or "experience your potential today." While these are not totally wrong it does suggest that the prime goal we should be pursuing is our own comfort and the experience of some form of self-expression rather than growth in the character and quality of the life of our Lord and Savior Jesus Christ. Someone said it this way, "Simply put, our modern day society, and this includes a great number of Christians, is focused on making satisfaction its goal, indeed, its religion. There is much more concern for self-fulfillment than for pleasing God and truly serving Him and others as seen in the life of Jesus." Let me once more emphasize that, while many of these things are important and have their place in our lives, they certainly take the focus off what is truly the heart of Christianity and this is knowing and loving God, and out of that resource and relationship, living as servants in the power of the Spirit according to the example of Christ.

Now let's also remember that when serving others and their needs, if the underlying motive and goal is some form of self love, like the praise of others for the service rendered, then that service is in reality hypocritical. This type of service is really aimed at serving selfish ends—usually in the futile pursuit of personal significance through something like praise, power, or status.

The real test of whether we are truly maturing and learning to have a Christ-like servant's heart, is how we act when people treat us like one.

As we look at what a servant heart is, let's look at:

The Hindrances of Servanthood

The desire to feel important is a tremendous barrier to what the Bible and what Jesus Christ taught about biblical servanthood. We see this in the reluctance of the disciples to take the towel and the position of a servant as we find in John 13 where we now find it is time for every Christian to take the towel.

Notice the following hindrances:

1. Wanting to meet our own felt needs pose a hindrance to being the servant that Christ wants of us.

I find that everyone faces the problem of meeting their felt needs by their own solutions and defense and escape mechanisms (i.e., the things people do to protect their self image or how they want people to feel about them), but our need and responsibility is to trust the Lord. It is the duty of every Christian not to seek to serve our own needs, but to accept the responsibility of becoming servants of others like the Lord.

CHAPTER THREE

2. Self-centered living or seeking happiness from the world will cause the Christian to fail to live as servants.

This naturally will result in a lack of surrender and having wrong priorities and goals which will leave little or no time for the Lord or His ministry to others and the body of Christ. This is a crucial area for the Christian to see the importance of Philippians 1:21, that says, *"For to me to live (to have life and existence) is Christ, and to die is gain."*

The Results in the Absence of Servanthood

1. The opposite of a servant's heart is self-seeking, and this will lead to jealousy, envy, disunity and division. Turn to Luke 22:24-30 and we see this all over again with the disciples. It was Leonard Bernstein, the celebrated orchestra conductor, was once asked, "What is the hardest instrument to play?" Without a moment's hesitation he replied, "Second fiddle. I can always get plenty of first violinists. But to find one who plays second violin with as much enthusiasm, or second French horn, or second flute, now that's a problem! And yet if no one plays second, *we have no harmony.*"

2. Failure to get involved in ministry is a close step to become as in the case of the disciples' behavior in John 13. The absence of a servant's heart causes people to just simply sit back and expect everyone else to serve them. A good example of this is found in Luke chapter 10 with Mary and Martha.

It is often true that we begin our ministry with the right motivation, but somehow we get off track. This appears to be what happened to Martha. In a very familiar story, found only in Luke's gospel,

GIVE ME AN OLD SHOE

Martha becomes greatly distressed in the midst of preparing a meal for Jesus as we find that some people suffer from "burn out" in the ministry. In this passage of Scripture, we find that Martha is "burned up" in hers. This woman is really angry, and with Jesus no less!

Who could think of a lovelier thing for a woman to be doing than to be showing Him the hospitality of a meal? And yet Martha virtually explodes with anger, due to the fact that her sister, Mary, is not helping, but rather is sitting at the feet of Jesus. And not only is Martha angry with her sister, she is greatly upset with her Lord. What happened to Martha's ministry? What went wrong with her motivation? Why was Martha mad at Jesus? The answers to these questions can be found only in God's Word.

The story of Martha and Mary underscores the futility of works as well. It was not the frantic activity of Martha which impressed Jesus, and which won His commendation, but the inactivity of Mary, sitting at the feet of the Savior, listening intently to His teaching. If one would place too high an emphasis on works, this story will put things back into perspective.

We find that Martha is very aggressive and outspoken. She explodes with anger at Mary's failure to come to her aid, and at Jesus' encouragement (or at least His toleration) of her conduct. All of the texts combined paint a picture of Martha as the older, the more dominant (and perhaps domineering), the more outgoing, and the more vocal of the two.

Martha was upset because Mary remained at Jesus' feet, listening to Him teach, while the burden of fixing the meal fell entirely on

CHAPTER THREE

her. What was Mary doing at Jesus' feet? How did she get there? I think I know.

LET'S LOOK AT MARY

As we study the Scriptures, we find that Mary was always at Jesus' feet. Indeed, in every text which speaks of her, she is at Jesus' feet. In Luke chapter 7 she was behind Jesus, quietly washing Jesus' feet with her tears and her hair. In John 11 she fell at Jesus' feet when she found Him. Mary, I believe, was at the feet of Jesus, doing what every good host or hostess would have done—washing the feet of their guest. It is my opinion that Mary just never got up. Mary was not content to make a quick job of it. Jesus began to speak, and she was captivated by His words. She was so inconspicuous, her actions so gracious, and Jesus so grateful and affirming, that she never thought of getting up and slipping away to the kitchen. I suspect that practically everyone else in that room could hear the murmuring of Martha, and the clanging of the pots and dishes as she proceeded to get "boiled" by the moment, but not Mary. She had eyes only for the One who had forgiven her, and who loved her, as she loved Him. She had no ears for Martha's clamoring, but only for the gracious words spoken by her Master. Was she normally subject to Martha? Not so today, and Jesus was grateful to have her at His feet. The warmth of the love of that woman must have caused the room to glow. Who would dare to suggest she leave, no matter what Martha might want?

LET'S LOOK AT MARTHA

There are several things about Martha that we should take note of, before we consider our Lord's words spoken to her.

1. **It is Martha who is the central person in our text, not Mary.**

We might all agree that Mary is the hero, she is the model, but she is not the dominant personality of our passage. Luke's account records not so much as one word spoken by Mary, and there is but one brief verse describing her actions (Luke 10:39). The remaining four verses are divided between Martha's actions (Luke 10: 38 & 40) and Jesus' response to Martha's tantrum (Luke 10:41-42).

2. **I believe that Martha was not jealous that Mary was spending time with Jesus, but angry that Mary was not helping her.**

One thing struck me as I have been thinking about Martha's response to Mary's actions: Martha was not envious of Mary, but angry with her. If Martha had said, "I would like to sit at your feet, too, Jesus," that would have been one thing. But Martha did not say this. Martha seems to have felt that working in the kitchen was the "better thing," not only for her, but also for Mary. How sad that Martha did not have the longing which Mary evidenced, the

CHAPTER THREE

longing to do nothing else than to sit at Jesus' feet, and to hear Him teach. Here was "bread" for which Martha had too little concern, or so it would seem.

3. **As most people are guilty of, Martha does not see any problem with herself, but she blames those who are innocent of wrongdoing.**

   Martha accused both Mary and Jesus of doing wrong against her, and thought of herself as innocent. Jesus refused to grant Martha's demands, even though forcefully put. Jesus praised Mary for the choice she had made and informed Martha that she was in the wrong.

4. **It is not Martha's service which was wrong, but her attitude in that service.**

   I do not think our text suggests that both Mary and Martha should have been sitting at Jesus' feet, and that no meal should have been prepared. Martha was not wrong in serving, but her attitude in serving was clearly wrong. Martha had a serving ministry, but not a servant's heart. As a Christian, we must have the right heart attitude in our serving in our Lord's ministry. If we are not careful, we may cause many to fall by the wayside with our attitude.

5. **I think that you will agree that Martha's frustration, anger, and temper tantrum may not be excusable, but it is at least understandable.**

   If Mary's delight at sitting at the Master's feet is easily understood, so is Martha's attitude. It is not excusable, but it is understandable. Let me remind you that Martha, as the hostess of the house, may well have been faced with entertaining a sizable group.

For many years my wife and I would have all of our children and their children and the grandkids and nieces and nephews for a special time at Christmas. At least 50 or 60 people were there for at least one meal. There was a great deal of planning and preparation involved. My wife played a large role in this, and she can testify to the work involved. I gather from this experience that Martha likewise had no mean job. She could have used all the help she could get.

Another factor in Martha's anger at Mary's absence may have been a cultural one. In that day and time (as is still often the case in the Eastern world) the men would sit about talking "man talk" like we men still do today, while the women were going about their more "domestic duties" for Mary to have been in the "living room and not in the "kitchen" may have been unusual. Martha may not have sensed the Lord's encouragement for Mary to stay, or, she may very well have observed it, which would explain her outburst of anger toward Him. Was she reminding Jesus of how He should "take the leadership" here?

6. **Martha's words reflect not only an anger, but a lack of reverence and a lack of submission.**

Martha charged Jesus with not caring for her, with condoning wrongdoing on Mary's part, and then publicly demanded that Jesus grant His "error" by making Mary go to help her sister. One must say that this is hardly proper conduct. If Martha thought that Mary was not conforming to her "womanly role" how much more so for herself.

CHAPTER THREE

SEE HOW JESUS RESPONDED TO MARTHA'S REBUKE

Jesus' words in response to the stormy protest of Martha may not tell us all that was wrong, but they surely inform us as to what the primary problem was. Notice several things about Jesus' words to Martha.

1. **Notice that Jesus did not respond to Martha's anger in anger.**

   How easy it would have been for you or I to have a scorching, or at least a sarcastic response to Martha, but no trace of anger can be seen by Jesus. Our Lord's response is truly gracious, and His rebuke most gentle. That same compassion, which drew Mary to Jesus' feet, is that which characterized Jesus' response to her sister and to us as well when we do not show a Christian attitude toward others.

2. **Again, notice that Jesus found Martha's charges wrong on every count and at the same time found Martha to be the one in the wrong.**

   Her tears and her rebuke, no matter how strongly put, do not put Jesus on the defensive. Jesus made no attempt to clear Himself, He defended Mary's decision as the better one, and found Martha's outburst unjustified, and a symptom of more serious problems. Angry accusations and outbursts, especially those which are not fair (as was that of Martha), often point to deeper spiritual problems. It is to these problems that our Lord's words will point.

3. **Again, Jesus' response was evidence of His refusal to show some kind of stereotypical "woman's role" model on Mary and Martha alike.**

   Mary and Martha were both women, but nothing in Jesus' words deals with either of them as women. Mary was not only free to sit and learn at Jesus' feet, she was commended for it. Martha was not forbidden or rebuked for serving, but only for insisting that Mary do likewise. Jesus dealt with these women as individuals.

4. **Look how closely Jesus dealt more with the attitudes of these women than He did their actions.**

   Martha was rebuked for her wrong attitudes of being "worried and upset." While Mary was motivated by love, gratitude, and pure joy, Martha was running on the steam of distress and consternation. This was not way to be serving her Lord.

5. **Then Jesus exposed the problem with Martha's priorities.**

   Mary had chosen that which was "better" and "necessary" (v. 42); Martha was upset and frustrated by a number of things ("many things," v. 41). What was that "better" thing, that which was "necessary," that which Mary had chosen, and Martha had not? In brief, I think that the "better thing" was abiding in Christ, in an attitude of worship, drawing strength and instruction from Him. It was being taught at the feet of the Master. If there is any one element of discipleship, it is being a learner, and this is what Mary had chosen to do. Martha was preoccupied with ministering to Jesus; Mary with the ministry of Jesus. In the final analysis, He is not dependent upon our ministry to Him, but our life in Him is totally dependent upon His ministry to us. In seeking to serve Jesus, Martha was hindering the sustenance of Jesus in her life, and she even demanded that it be kept from her sister as well.

CHAPTER THREE

6. Finally, Jesus exposed a problem of responsibilities.

Martha had greatly overstepped her areas of responsibility. Simply put, Martha was responsible only for her attitude, for her service. Martha had extended her responsibility to "many things," things which were not hers to assume. She felt responsible to direct Mary's ministry, and even to dictate our Lord's responsibilities (by demanding He correct Mary). She had begun to assume responsibility for others.

We should first seek to understand this event and its meaning in the context of Luke's gospel. What is the Spirit of God teaching us here, at this point in Luke's developing argument of the life of Christ? I believe that this story illustrates many of the things which Luke has been emphasizing up to this point, as well as correcting any possible misconceptions. I believe that Luke is, by means of this incident, illustrating what true discipleship is. The essence of discipleship is not our service rendered to Christ, but finding our sustenance in Christ. It is not being a Martha, but a Mary. Discipleship is not so much a teeth-gritting devotion to duty, as a joyful devotion to and dependence on Christ.

Our story is also further evidence of the priorities which characterize our Lord and which should characterize His disciples. One of these priorities is that of being sustained and strengthened by the Word of God as opposed to finding our strength from earthly sustenance, namely food. In the temptation of our Lord by Satan to command stones to become bread, our Lord's response was, "It is written, 'Man does not live on bread alone'" (Luke 4:4). But how can we say that being in the Word is more important, "better," than serving Him? We can say this because abiding in Christ through His Word provides us with both the motivation and the means for serving Him. Service may not result in the study of God's Word, but honest searching of Scripture will produce service. Just as a branch cannot produce fruit by any other means than by abiding in the vine, so we cannot produce fruit apart from abiding in Christ through His Word.

I believe that Martha's explosive reaction to Mary's failure to join her in the kitchen is indicative of a very serious problem in her life. I believe that her problem may be summed up in this way: ***MARTHA WAS WRONG IN MEASURING HER SIGNIFICANCE IN TERMS OF HER SERVICE.***

Martha felt that her service was so vital that she could demand that Mary come to help her, even though it meant not being there to learn at the feet of the Savior. Martha was so violent in her response that she accused the Lord of wrongdoing by not giving her the "support" she needed in her ministry.

I do not think that Martha would have been so touchy about her ministry if she did not have her "meaning in life" invested in it. The kitchen was the one area which was under Martha's authority. Martha was so involved in preparing meals and offering hospitality that she saw herself as having value to others. When Jesus' actions threatened her ability to perform in this area, she strongly reacted. Martha found her ministry to be of too much value to her. She could not put it aside for anything, not even in order to learn at Jesus' feet. And she could not allow Mary to set it aside, either.

It is amazing that while Christians have come to the point of renouncing their performance, their works, as having anything to contribute to their salvation; they somehow think that their ministry does determine their significance to God, or at least to others. The Scriptures simply do

CHAPTER THREE

not teach this, for our spiritual gifts, our ministries, and our level of effectiveness are all sovereignty given us by God (1 Corinthians 12:4-6). The one who has a great ministry cannot take the credit, any more than the one with a seemingly insignificant ministry can take any blame. It is only required that we be faithful in using that which God has given us, in the context in which He has placed us.

I find it interesting to note that when our significance is not measured by our service, we are willing to accept either "success" or apparent "failure" in ministry as from God. John the Baptist rejoiced in the demise of his ministry, because he had played out his role, and the Master was being magnified. Paul dealt with many reverses in his life, and yet he was able to see them as from the hand of His sovereign Lord, and he could rejoice, even in the worst of circumstances (cf. Acts 16:25; 2 Corinthians 6; Philippians).

Our Lord's words to Martha inform us that the magnitude of our ministry is not nearly as important as the motivation of our ministry. It will not be until the day of judgment that the motives of men will be revealed, and thus our ministries should not be judged by us now (cf. 1 Corinthians 4:1-5). Let us beware of seeking to appraise the value of our ministries, since this is something which only God can judge with accuracy.

There is yet one final thing that I wish to say as I close. There is no better place to be, than at the feet of our Lord. When we fall at His feet, we acknowledge His majesty, power, and goodness, and our need. When we fall at His feet, we rightly reflect the response of the creature to the Creator. No sinner in the New Testament that I am aware of ever hesitated to come to Jesus' feet. The self-righteous would not be caught dead there, because of their pride and arrogance, but the sinner found the feet of Jesus a place of welcome. You are always welcome at His feet.

As you have looked at these consequences, the important question is, **do I have the heart of a servant**? If I think I do, then, in **what ways is it demonstrated in my life**?

_____
_____
_____
_____
_____
_____
_____

How Do We Develop the Heart of a Servant?

Humility as our Lord did. (Philippians. 2:5-8). The ultimate goal for Christians is to reflect the life of Christ in their own lives and the character trait that best enables us to do so, is humility. From this passage we find three things about our Lord that is the model for us:

1. He took the form of a servant. A humble leader does not boast of his authority, he or she identifies with the weakest member of the team.

2. He demonstrated humility through obedience to God the Father. A humble servant does not impose his or her will on God, but surrenders to God's command.

3. He waited for His Father to lift Him up. A servant doesn't grab for power or position.

CHAPTER THREE

Two elements to living as servants are ***surrender*** and ***sacrifice*** as are found in the exhortation of Romans 12:1-2.

Any true success we experience as servants will flow from surrender and sacrifice. The question is, are you a servant of Christ, if not why not renew your surrender in the following ways:

1. Quality relationships are founded on the foundation of surrender, first to God and then to others.

2. Practice servant hood by looking at and practicing Matthew 16:24-26.

Finally, it also means caring about people and getting to know them personally so we can help meet their particular needs as we are given opportunity.

WHY NOT GIVE YOURSELF AWAY; IT REALLY PAYS OFF, IN ETERNAL DIVIDENDS.

In your personal life, what areas can you give of yourself in the service to others?

1._____

2._____

3._____

4._____

5._____

ॐ 4 ॐ

~ Servanthood ~

"WHO WE ARE"

GIVE ME AN OLD SHOE

‏☙

T*he* Bible is very clear that at some point in the future, "every knee will bow at the name of Jesus." But as we study the New Testament, Jesus came to this earth to be a servant and what I am about to say, many of our "saved church members" do not like to hear is, Christ expects us to be servants and to serve Him and in turn to serve others.

Now the question is, "how does a Christian know whether he or she is really genuinely serving?"

Well, the best test is to ask yourself the following question: "have you grown as a person?" "Have you, while being served, become wiser as a Christian, wiser and more desirous of becoming a servant?" Now the best example to follow in this is the Master, Jesus Christ Himself. You will find in Mark chapter 10:35-45 how He didn't just talk about serving, He lived it out every day, in fact that was the reason that He came to earth was to serve God and through His death and resurrection to serve mankind.

CHAPTER FOUR

If you do a good study on the disciples and their ministry during their time with the Christ and His ministry, but also after Christ went back to Heaven, you will find that their ministry was one of being a "servant first of all."

As a Christian, life is a life of service, according to Colossians 3:16-17, we find four things that give us direction to be the Lord's servants.

1. *"Let the word of Christ dwell in you richly..."*

If you really want victory and how to be a servant, listen to the words of Paul in Romans 11:33, "Oh, the depth of the riches both of the wisdom and knowledge of God!" The background of verses one through thirty two, caused the apostle to break out in praise. Let's do a little in-depth study for a moment.

    a) Write down the word **"wisdom"** and turn to Psalm 104:24 and let the Word speak to your heart about His wisdom.

    _____
    _____
    _____
    _____

    b) *"How manifold are thy works! When we contemplate the wonderful works of Nature, and walking about at leisure, gaze upon this open theatre of the world, considering the stately beauty, constant order, and sumptuous furniture thereof; the glorious splendor and uniform motion of the heavens; the pleasant fertility of the earth; the curious figure and fragrant sweetness of plants; the exquisite frame of animals; and all other amazing miracles of nature, wherein are the glorious attributes of*

God, especially His transcendent goodness, are more conspicuously displayed: so that by them, not only large acknowledgments, but even gratulatory hymns, as it were, of praise have been extorted from the mouths of Aristotle, Pliny, Galen, and such like men, never suspected guilty of an excessive devotion; then should our hearts be affected with thankful sense, and our lips break forth in praise." --William Barrow, 1754-1836.

How does the quote above, help you as a servant?

_____
_____

c) Verse 24 -- *He does not undertake to answer his own question, "How manifold?"*

Here we find that he confesses God's works to be greater than his own power of expression; whether these "works" belong to the creation of nature or to that of grace. And observe how the concurrent operation of the Blessed Trinity is set forth when we read: "O Lord, how manifold are thy works," teaches of the Father, the Source of all things: "in wisdom hast thou made them all," tells of the Son, the Eternal Word, "Christ the power of God, and the Wisdom of God, by whom were all things made, and without him was not anything made that was made," (1 Corinthians 1:24; John 1:3); "the earth is full of thy riches," is spoken of the Holy Ghost, who filleth the world. -- Augustine, Hugo, and Uassiodorus, in Neale and Littledale.

CHAPTER FOUR

Can we not see that the language of God's wonder and wisdom is displayed and how important God's Word should be instilled in us as His servants?

2. *"In all wisdom, teaching and admonishing one another..."* Two truths here:

   a) When God's Word is dwelling in you and giving you greater understanding of His Word, then we are to do everything we can to pass it along to other believers.

   b) We are to share this truth of His Word to the unsaved.

3. *"In psalms and hymns and spiritual songs, singing with grace in your hearts to the Lord."* Think about this part of the verse for a moment. This is *worship!* One has said, *"You are never qualified to serve until you first worship your Lord."* Let's stop here for just a moment.

   a) **Why is worship important**?

   I believe that worship is rendering Lordship to Christ and worship is vital to the servant life now and in eternity. According to 1 Corinthians 13:9-10, worship will occupy our lives and hearts forever.

   b) **What is worship?**

   It certainly is not a sermon, which is a part of drawing us to worship, but a sermon is not worship, neither is praying or church music. Worship to me is "rendering Lordship." We are told in Psalms 99:5 to "exalt the Lord our God and worship at His footstool for He is holy." Worship exalts God and humbles man and in worship there is no room for hypocrisy, arrogance or pride.

GIVE ME AN OLD SHOE

> ***"You are never qualified to serve until you first worship your Lord."***

4. *"And whatever you do…":*

   a) *"in word"*-- whether it is teaching a Sunday school lesson or reading the Bible to some shut-in or in the hospital to the sick or dying soul.

   b) *"or deed"*-- this could be to cook a meal for someone, clean their house, cut the grass, repair some household needs, power washing the outside of their home, but mainly sharing the good news with a lost person.

   c) *"do all in the name of the Lord Jesus"*-- no matter how trained you are in God's Word and presentation, it must be done in His name.

   d) *"giving thanks to God the Father through Him"*-- there is no task too large or too small done in His name.

Every born again believer is to serve his Lord and Master, Jesus Christ. Paul makes this very clear in Romans 12:1, that we are *"bought with a price and we are not our own."* So then, the life of the servant is *one of total surrender* and we find this wonderful truth emphasized in 1 Corinthians 3:8-15. **What are those Crowns?**

CHAPTER FOUR

1. **The Crown of Life - James 1:12.**

   All believers, the saved, have eternal life, but not all believers have this crown. This crown will be given to those who are "faithful until death" (Revelation 2:10). This crown is for the believers who endure all manner of temptations and live for Christ faithfully and are surrendered wholly unto His Word and Service.

2. **The Crown Imperishable - 1 Corinthians 9:24-27.** This deals with denying of self for example:

   a) The believer must keep his eyes on Christ and not this world.

   b) The believer must look for his strength only in the Lord.

   c) The believer must surrender all on the altar.

   d) The believer must always, by faith, refuse anything that would hinder his spiritual progress.

3. **The Crown of Rejoicing - 1 Thessalonians 2:19.** This is the soul winner's crown. Why is this crown so important?

   a) It is the great cause for joy in heaven.

   b) It is the attack on sin to win souls.

   c) It is wise to win souls.

   d) How can one witness for Christ?

   > With your life that others will see Christ in you. How does your personal family see Christ in you at home or in public?

   How does your church family see you when you are not as faithful to church as you know and they know you should be?

- ➢ By witnessing with your mouth and trusting the Holy Spirit to give you the words to say and power to say them with. When was the last time that you asked even the simplest question to someone who has just waited on you at a restaurant, "is there anything that I can pray for you?"

- ➢ By giving your tithes and offerings that others may preach Christ.

4. The Crown of Righteousness - 2 Timothy 4:5-8.

We must not confuse "the righteousness of God" when we receive Christ as our Savior. The crown of righteousness is for the believer that is looking for and loves the second coming of Christ and this will affect their life until Christ comes for the church. This crown will be given at the Judgment Seat of Christ, how important is it for the Christian to look for the second coming of Christ (2 Corinthians 5:10).

5. The Crown of Glory - 1 Peter 5:2-4.

This crown is a special reward for the obedient, God-called, faithful pastors. I believe that every believer may share in this crown (Matthew 10:41). As a layperson, you are to support your pastor by praying for him and being an encourager in the work of the Lord. It is important that you undergird his ministry with your tithes and offerings and freely giving your time to the Lord's service as well, and God will reward you for your support of His chosen servant. For the pastor, he will earn his reward by:

a) Preaching the Word without fear or favor and when it is necessary, to "convince, rebuke, exhort with all longsuffering and teaching" (2 Timothy 4:1-5).

CHAPTER FOUR

b) By taking the spiritual oversight of the church. Every God called pastor is responsible to God for the message preached to his people. He is not to please the membership, but to please His God.

c) He is to be an example to the church and to his community that he serves. It is time that the church have a leader he or she can depend on and have confidence in and to follow. It is time to have a world that can have a leader they can trust in all areas of life.

As we have seen, every believer will be rewarded according to his own labor, but we must understand that we do not labor for salvation (Ephesians 2:8-9), for salvation is by the completed work of Jesus Christ on the cross and his glorified resurrection. It is also true that the believer has a choice of two types of materials to build on, "eternal materials" or "temporal materials" (see 2 Corinthians 4:18).

So then in conclusion a True Servant:

1. Puts others ahead of himself.

2. Possesses the confidence to serve.

3. Serves to encourage others.

4. Serves because of love for Christ, His ministry and to help others.

5. Performs small acts and does not ask for recognition.

6. Learns people and their needs.

GIVE ME AN OLD SHOE

Dear reader, what are you building on?

_____

_____

_____

> *"Every born again believer is to serve his Lord and Master, Jesus Christ."*

5

~ Servanthood ~

"THE DESIRE ~ HOW TO SERVE"

GIVE ME AN OLD SHOE

○○

*H*ow does this work? Good question. Turn to Revelation chapter five and verses one through fourteen and you will find the description of our exalted Savior in which we find a magnificent picture of the highest position held by our risen Lord. Now to refer to Christ merely as a "leader" might sound to you and I rather a demeaning one but to call Him a "servant!" Why such a label might be *"blasphemous"*----were it not for the fact that Christ went to such unspeakable lengths to achieve that very lowly title.

In Isaiah chapter fifty-three, we find the prophecy that God's own Son would be the Suffering Servant for all men. And when you read the gospels, you will find that Jesus lived His life as the definitive statement about serving as the path to greatness (Matthew 20:28). If you look closely at the writings of the apostle Paul, you will see Jesus identified as the ultimate example of a servant (Philippians 2:5-7).

CHAPTER FIVE

It is absolutely correct to say that no one else has ever influenced the world as a servant, as Jesus Christ did and still does and according to Scripture. So as a Christian, no one can or could argue with following His command, because He became the great example of every kind of service that He ever commanded. And today, He still models greatness as the ultimate servant-leader.

In His sacrifice on the cross, Jesus provided us with the ultimate illustration of servant leadership. Christ took our infirmities and carried our sorrows and if we believe this, what prevents us from serving others as He has served us?

What do we have to believe about God and ourselves in order to fully embrace a servant leadership mindset?

For you and I to be the servant we are to be is to follow the example of our Savior and what an example, but it will be in the area of "humility."

Let's take a few moments to look at this subject of "humility." In Isaiah 66:2, we read, "This is the one I esteem: he who is humble and contrite in spirit and trembles at my word." As one reads God's Word, they will find repeatedly emphasized, that God opposes the proud but gives grace to the humble. The proud have an inappropriate and much inflated view of themselves. Because of this they attribute accomplishments to their own efforts, and knowledge and fail to give everything they have to God.

It is time that Christians come to the point in life today that they are in desperate need for the grace and mercy of God, to develop a teachable spirit and seek wise counsel and to be willing to be under the authority of God.

Paul says it this way, "let each of you look out not only for his own interests, but also for the interests of others" (Philippians 2:3-4).

GIVE ME AN OLD SHOE

Well how does this humility work? How can the Christian that is successful maintain humility? Let's see what Solomon said about this subject by turning to Proverbs 25:27. Many leaders just love being in charge, making decisions that affect the organization or church if you please, delegating and implementing the decisions to others, in other words, "running the show." Someone once said, "It is not good...to set one's own honor. Doing so is like eating too much honey. Sweet as it is, and healthy as it is in proper amounts, too much of a good thing will make you sick---and sick of it."

Honor accompanies a job well done. If a person who has to go looking for honor, that person has his or her hand in the wrong hive. We find that Solomon learned that focusing on a job well done is the way to earn honor. Focusing on honor cuts into the time and energy needed to do the job well. "It is not honorable to seek your own honor." Doing so will make you a "sick" servant.

Now then, as a servant, what are we to do? What can we learn? The main goal for servant leaders is to reflect the life of Christ in our own lives. Paul in Philippians 2:5-11 tells us how to follow the example of Christ where we learn three things about our Lord that is our model.

1. Our Lord did not selfishly cling to the outer expression of His divinity. Instead, He took the form of a servant and the servant leader doesn't flaunt his or her position or power. Instead, he or she identifies with the weakest member of the team. How can one do this?

_____
_____
_____

CHAPTER FIVE

2. Jesus demonstrated servanthood through obedience to God the Father. A Servant doesn't impose his will on God, but submits to God's commands. How does one submit to God's commands?

   _____
   _____
   _____
   _____

3. Jesus waited for His Father to lift Him up. A servant doesn't grab for power or position. He or she will wait patiently for God to increase their influence.

> *"If a person has to go looking for honor, his or her hand is in the wrong hive."*

GIVE ME AN OLD SHOE

Where do you stand on these three examples?

_____
_____
_____

Let's continue with this thought about Jesus being a servant. Servanthood has become something of a weakness and passivity in our churches today. Because Jesus knew who He was, He was secure enough to serve others. Let's look at John 13:4 and see what this really tells us to do as we serve others.

Here we find a beautiful picture of the Lord's Supper with all of them around the table, but we find a more beautiful picture of how the Son of God took a towel, when He could have taken a sword or a scepter and become a king, but Jesus took a towel and became the servant. This lesson was very appropriate, for the disciples were quarreling as who would be chief and the greatest among them. Not much has changed today in the circles of Christianity. When one of these men should have stood up and took the towel, not one was willing to take the servants place. When they wanted to take a throne, He was willing to take a towel.

What most Christians today do not see is that, to the basin and the towel and the disciples' feet, no artist can paint that. As you read that story in God's Word, may it melt your heart with wonder and awe that He, who was so very high, would stoop so very low. What an example of a humble servant. Yes, Jesus knew He was to serve others, how does your understanding of your identity relate to the example of the one who gave Himself for our sins?

The question now is how can I serve without becoming proud? The Bible message is that God is telling us, "I am God, and you are not." Peter tells

CHAPTER FIVE

us to "Humble yourselves, therefore under God's mighty hand that He may lift you up." Ask God for the grace to make this passage a reality in your life. It is when we come to grips with our desperate need for the grace and mercy of God, we will develop a teachable spirit and seek wise counsel and be under His authority.

Some leaders lead from a domineering and often arrogant "top-down" framework because it is traditional, is the most common, is the easiest, and comes naturally. However, this may not be the most effective form of leadership in order to produce the best work environment for everyone. It may also not be the most efficient for making an organization more efficient and furthering the organization's mission, vision, and core values. A different type of leadership that may be better effective at doing these things is servant leadership. Servant leadership opposes "top-down," autocratic leadership. A servant leader acts as a steward to the organization's financial, human, and other resources. Servant leadership emphasizes trust, empathy, collaboration, and the ethical use of power. At the heart of servant leadership, the individual leader of a church program or an organization is a servant first. He or she makes a conscious decision to lead in order to better serve others, not to increase his or her own power. The servant leader's objective is to enhance the growth of individuals in the organization and increase teamwork and personal involvement.

Becoming a servant leader should first involve you making the choice of service over self-interest. True leadership emerges from those whose primary motivation is a deep desire to help others.

You must understand that servant leadership is a transformational, long-term approach to work and life, a way of being that has the potential for creating positive change throughout our society.

GIVE ME AN OLD SHOE

Become familiar with the principles of servant leadership and try to incorporate them into your leadership style as you grow as a leader: transformation as a vehicle for personal and institutional growth; personal growth as a route to better serve others; enabling environments that empower and encourage service; service as a fundamental goal; trusting relationships as a basic platform for collaboration and service; creating commitment as a way to collaborative activity; community building as a way to create environments in which people can trust each other and work together; nurturing the spirit as a way to provide joy and fulfillment in meaningful work.

Try to emulate and incorporate the following characteristics that are pivotal to servant leadership, merging them into your own leadership style: empathy, listening, awareness, healing, persuasion, foresight, stewardship, conceptualization, community building, and commitment to the growth of people.

Understand that the ideals of servant leadership can be implemented both at an individual level as a means for personal growth (such as for professional, intellectual, emotional, and spiritual growth), and at the organizational level as a means for a more effective mission, vision, core values, and guiding philosophy, creating better, more productive and profitable, and more caring companies and institutions.

The life of service requires total commitment. Christian services are of and by the Holy Spirit; therefore, they are spiritually discerned. If you are not born again, this lesson to you is foolishness. "For the message of the cross is foolishness to those who are perishing, but to us who are being saved it is the power of God" (1 Corinthians 1:18).

The Christian life is a life of service that will be rewarded here on earth and in heaven.

CHAPTER FIVE

What is your desire and what is holding you back?

_____
_____
_____

Why not take time here to reflect on the desires to serve your Lord and how you can?

_____
_____
_____
_____
_____

6

~ Servanthood ~
"THE ABILITY TO SERVE"

CHAPTER SIX

*S*omeone said about Character this way: *"Leadership is the capacity and will to rally men to a common purpose and the character which inspires confidence."*

Let's look briefly at the abilities of a servant.

1. How a servant deals with the circumstances of life tells you many things about his character. Crisis doesn't necessarily make character, but it certainly does reveal it.

2. We choose our character. In fact, we create it every time we make choices.

3. The respect that servanthood must have requires that one's ethics be without question. A leader not only stays above the line, between right and wrong, he stays well clear of the "gray-areas."

GIVE ME AN OLD SHOE

Charisma: "How can you have charisma? Be more concerned about making others feel good about themselves than you are about making them feel good about you."

1. I have yet to find the man who does better work and puts forth greater effort under a spirit of approval than under a spirit of criticism.

2. Charisma is the ability to draw people to you.

3. People enjoy leaders/servants that love and are passionate about life.

4. One of the best things you can do for people is to expect the best of them.

5. It has been proven that highly successful people could only see the good in people and the greatest good you can do for another is not just share your riches but to reveal to him his own.

6. *It is a fact that hope* is greatest of all possessions, and as you serve people and give of yourself to share wisdom, resources, and even special occasions.

Commitment: "People do not follow uncommitted leaders."

1. The world has never seen a great servant who lacked commitment. The Law of Buy-in states that people buy into the servant, then the vision.

2. Some people want everything to be perfect before they're willing to commit themselves to anything. But commitment always precedes achievement.

3. The only real measure of commitment by a servant is action.

4. There will be times when commitment is the only thing that carries a servant forward.

CHAPTER SIX

5. Let's look at Acts 20:29-38.

Communication: "Communicators take something complicated and make it simple."

1. Servants must be able to share knowledge and ideas to transmit a sense of urgency and enthusiasm to others.

2. Communication is not just what you say. It's also how you say it. The key to effective communication is simplicity.

3. Speeches - Exciting opening, dramatic summary, as close together as possible.

4. To become a better communicator, become audience-oriented. People believe in great communicators because great communicators believe in people.

5. First, believe in what you say. Second, live what you say.

6. As you communicate, never forget that the goal of communication is action.

"Leadership is the capacity and will to rally men to a common purpose and the character which inspires confidence."

GIVE ME AN OLD SHOE

Competence: "Competence is the servant's ability to say it, plan it, and do it in such a way that others know that you know how – and know that they want to follow you."

1. Competent people come ready to play every day, no matter what the circumstances they face.

2. All highly competent people continually search for ways to keep learning, growing, and improving.

3. The person, who knows how, will always have a job, but the person who knows why will always be the servant.

4. Quality is never an accident: it is always the result of high intention, sincere effort, intelligent direction, and skillful execution. It represents the wise choice of many alternatives.

Courage: "One person with courage is a majority." This is vital to a servant.

1. "Courage is rightly esteemed the first of human qualities, because it is the quality which guarantees all others."

2. "Courage is fear that has said its prayers."

3. Courage is doing what you're afraid to do. There can be no courage unless you're scared.

4. Courage isn't an absence of fear. A member of my church said this, "It's doing what you're afraid to do." It's having the power to let go of the familiar and forge ahead into new territory.

CHAPTER SIX

5. The ultimate measure of a man is not where he stands in moments of comfort and convenience, but where he stands at times of challenge and controversy.

6. Courage deals with principle, not perception. If you don't have the ability to see when to stand up and the conviction to do it, you'll never be an effective servant in all areas of life.

7. "Courage is contagious." – "Fear limits a servant."

8. "Fear not that your life will come to an end, but that it will never have a beginning."

I found this saying interesting, *"What's ironic is that those who don't have the courage to take risks and those who do, experience the same amount of fear in life."*

Discernment: "Smart servant/leaders believe only half of what they hear. Discerning leaders know which half to believe."

1. Discernment - "The ability to find the root of the matter, and it relies on intuition as well as rational thought."

2. "Nothing in life is to be feared, only to be understood."

3. Discernment enables the servant to see a partial picture, fill in the missing pieces intuitively, and find the real heart of the matter.

4. The closer a servant is to his area of his gift, the stronger his intuition and ability to see root causes. If you want to tap into your discernment potential, work in your areas of strength. This is why you must seek just what is your spiritual gift.

5. "Never ignore a gut feeling, but never believe that it's enough."

    Focus: "If you chase two rabbits, both will escape." What does this mean? _____
_____

1. What does it take to have the focus required to be a truly effective servant? A servant is one that knows his Priorities and has Concentration.

2. "Don't major in minors."

3. The great mystery isn't that people do things badly but that they occasionally do a few things well. Strength is always specific!

4. Growth equals change. If you want to get better, you have to keep changing and improving. That means stepping out into new areas.

5. Work on yourself, on your priorities, in your strengths, and with your companions.

    Generosity: "No person was ever honored for what he received. Honor has been the reward for what he gave." Just look at the following and let them sink in to you as a servant.

1. Giving is the highest level of living.

2. It's hard for a person to be generous when he is not satisfied with what he has. Generosity rises out of contentment, and that doesn't come with acquiring more.

3. If you're not content with little, you won't be content with a lot. And if you're not generous with little, you won't suddenly change if you become wealthy.

CHAPTER SIX

4. The measure of a leader is not the number of people who serve him, but the number of people he serves. Generosity requires putting others first.

5. The only way to really win with money is to hold it loosely-and be generous with it to accomplish things of value. "Money is a wonderful servant but a terrible master. If it gets on top and you get under it, you will become its slave."

6. "You have not lived today until you have done something for someone who can never repay you."

7. "All that is not given is lost."

Initiative: "Success seems to be connected with action. Successful people keep moving. They make mistakes, but they don't quit."

1. Of all the things a servant should fear, complacency should be at the very front of his life.

2. Servants are responsible for initiating a connection with those they are leading. But that's not the only area where servants must show initiative. They must always look for opportunities and be ready to take action such as Christ did when He took the lead to serve the disciples.

3. "The starting point of all achievement is desire." If you're going to be an effective servant, you've got to know what you want. That's the only way you'll recognize opportunity when it comes.

Listening: "The ear of the servant must be in tune with the voices of the people."

1. "A good servant encourages those he leads to tell him what he needs to know, not what he wants to hear."

GIVE ME AN OLD SHOE

2. Servants touch a heart before they ask for a hand. But before a servant can touch a person's heart, he has to know what's in it. One learns this by listening.

Passion: "Anyone can dabble, but once you've made that commitment, it's very hard for people to stop you."

1. Concentrate on what you do well, and do it better than anybody else.

2. "Nobody can be successful unless he loves his work."

3. Passion makes it possible for people who might seem ordinary to achieve great things.

4. Your desire determines your destiny. Anyone who lives beyond an ordinary life has great desire.

5. There is no substitute for passion. It is fuel for the servant to go on to do his best. If you want anything badly enough, you can find the willpower to achieve it.

6. If you follow your passion, instead of others' perceptions, you can't help becoming a more dedicated, productive servant. And you will find that increases your ability to impact other lives for Christ. In the end, your passion will have more influence than your personality.

Positive Attitude: "A successful man is one who can lay a firm foundation with the bricks others have thrown at him."

The Law of Magnetism really is true. Dr. Curtis Hutson said many years ago, when I had him for a meeting at our church, ***"you don't attract what you want, you attract what you are."*** *I have, for over forty-three years in the ministry, tied to live up to this statement as a servant of my Lord Jesus Christ.*

CHAPTER SIX

Relationships: "The most important single ingredient in the formula of success, is knowing how to get along with people."

1. It has been said, and I know from experience as a pastor, "People don't care how much you know until they know how much you care."

2. People truly do want to go along with people they get along with. And while someone can have people skills and not be a good leader, he cannot be a good leader without people skills.

3. The first quality of a relational servant is the ability to understand how people feel and think.

4. The ability to look at each person, understand him, and connect with him is a major factor in personal relationships.

5. I have found that people respect a servant who keeps their interests in mind.

> *"You don't attract what you want, you attract what you are."*

GIVE ME AN OLD SHOE

Responsibility: "Success on any major scale requires you to accept responsibility… In the final analysis, the one quality that all successful people have is the ability to take on responsibility."

If you have trouble achieving excellence, maybe you've lowered your standards. Dr. Lee Robertson, great pastor, educator and preacher once told me when I was a young pastor and struggling with leadership and servanthood, "everything rises and falls on leadership." I knew then that I had to have standards higher than any of the members that I was pastoring then, and after forty-three years in the ministry I still hold to this principle.

Security: "No man will make a great leader who wants to do it all himself or get all the credit for doing it."

Self-Discipline: "The first and best victory is to conquer self." How do you fit in this area and what do you need to do about it? Can you give a Scripture verse that addresses this statement?

Let me give you some hints and find the scriptures for these verses:

"For to me _____ is gain."

_____.

"He must_____ but I must _____"

_____.

The bottom line is this about Servanthood: ***"You've got to love your people, ministry and Savior more than your position."***

1. Servanthood is not about position or skill. It's about attitude.

2. The truth is that the best leaders desire to serve others, not themselves.

CHAPTER SIX

3. A good definition is this: Intentionally being aware of people's need, be available to help them, and able to accept their desires as important.

4. The real heart of servanthood is security. Listen to this true statement, "show me someone who thinks he is too important to serve, and I'll show you someone who is basically insecure."

5. It is true that those who would be great must be like the least and be the servant of all.

Teach Ability: *"It's what you learn after you know it all that counts."* Former great basketball coach, John Wooden

Vision: "A servant's courage to fulfill his vision comes from passion, not position."

What is the definition of passion? _____
_____
_____
_____

> *"You've got to love your people, ministry and Savior more than your position."*

༄ 7 ༀ

~ Servanthood ~
"BEING A GIVER"

The question is this, how can we hope to measure up to the Son of God as a servant? Can regular people, Christians, become true servants as well? Follow with me to the book of Acts (Acts 4:34-37).

In these verses we found a great servant-leader, Barnabas. Barnabas was one of the church's all-time great servant-leaders and in the above verses we find why he was such a servant "giver." One has said, "He believed that he existed for the good of the church more than he believed that the church existed to serve him and meet his needs."

Well, we know that he was a man who wanted to do what was right and this came early in his Christian birth and he became one who wanted to be discipled.

CHAPTER SEVEN

What do we know about Barnabas?
Acts 4:34-37

We also know that Barnabas was a man who was very generous. He did more than just make a token contribution to early church. We find that he sold some real estate and gave the money to the apostles. "Having land, sold it, and brought the money, and laid it at the apostles' feet," (Acts 4:37).

We also know that he was a man who had a special talent, he was called the "Son of Consolation or Encouragement."

It is interesting to note that his name matched his most outstanding characteristic. What if our name matched our most outstanding characteristic? For instance my first name means *"Well born,"* the second means, *"bright minded"* and my last name means *"shelter or scholar."* Do I match up to these characteristics? Well, let's don't go there! Let's get back to the important part of this lesson and see how Barnabas came to have this name? I believe, it was based on Scripture, because he was willing to stand beside others to be an encourager.

Let's look at some of those that he stood beside and how he became the servant that he was.

GIVE ME AN OLD SHOE

We'll get back to Barnabas in a little while. For the moment, let's look at his spiritual gift. Romans 12:8 says, "If it (a person's gift) is encouraging, let him encourage." The Greek word is very interesting. It is *parakaleo*. **Para** is a preposition meaning *"alongside of"* and *kaleo* is a verb meaning *"to call."* So **parakaleo** means *"to call alongside of."* It has the idea of coming to the aid or assistance of someone else. In particular, it implies an ability to help someone in an area where he cannot help himself.

It's the picture of a weary traveler stumbling down the highway with a heavy load on his shoulders. His head is bending low; his shoulders are now stooped, his knees become wobbly, and his feet barely moving. Each step he takes is agony. As you watch him, he begins to stagger and then he begins to fall. So you rush from your place, come alongside and you lift the load from his shoulders and place it on your own. Then you put your arm around him and say, "It's all right. I'll help you make it." And together you walk on down the road. That's **parakaleo**. It's coming alongside another person to help him in his moment of need.

There is a business near Raeford, NC, and Fayetteville, NC, that is called the *"Paraclete."* This is where those that want to know the experience of jumping out of an airplane, gets to do so without doing it in reality. Here the instructor goes alongside of the one looking for the experience and gives them support. The person who does that is called a *paraclete*. That's the Greek word used in John 14:16 for the Holy Spirit and in 1 John 2:1 for the Lord Jesus Christ. In the first case, the word means that the Holy Spirit comes alongside to give us strength to live the Christian life. In the latter case, it means that the Lord Jesus is our Advocate who speaks up in our defense.

CHAPTER SEVEN

So this gift could be called exhortation or comfort or encouragement. It is the divine ability to lift the load from a brother or sister and help them along the way. What an opportunity for the servant to be available in times like these.

There are at least two places in the New Testament where all Christians are commanded to encourage each other. 1Thessalonians 5:11 says, "Therefore, comfort each other and edify one another, just as you also are doing." Hebrews 3:13 says, "But exhort one another daily." This work of load-lifting is something all of us are to perform for each other as we see the need and have the opportunity.

The spiritual gift simply means that some of us will have a special ability in this area. In our 301 class that I teach here at Mid-Way Baptist Church, we call this gift "Exhortation" and define it this way: It is the special ability God gives to certain members of the body of Christ which enables them to come alongside another person to give encouragement, challenge, counsel or earnest advice as needed in such a way that the person is helped. That last phrase is worth pondering—"in such a way that the person is helped." Let's face it, I like what one pastor said "There are too many people, whose definition of encouragement is backing up the dump truck, pulling the lever and unloading on somebody. That's not encouragement; it's just dumping on people."

How Can We Spot This Gift?

When a person with this gift of encouragement spends time with you, you inevitably feel better. Even if they are counseling you about some weakness in your life, their words somehow make you stronger.

GIVE ME AN OLD SHOE

Here are a few other marks of the gifted load-lifters:

1. They genuinely like people.

2. They are strongly relational.

3. They always cheer for the underdog.

4. They are open-minded, forgiving and tolerant.

5. They are quick to respond to human needs.

6. They are quick to give the benefit of the doubt.

7. They are usually well-liked by others.

8. They are talkative.

9. They are quick to spot spiritual potential.

10. They are good coalition-builders.

> *"That's not encouragement; it's just dumping on people."*

CHAPTER SEVEN

How many of these characteristics fit you? Why not list them now?

_____
_____
_____
_____
_____

I thought the following was a great way to describe an encourager.

➢ This is the "How-to" gift. People who have it are hands-on, practical types. They don't like a lot of theory and get bored with doctrinal discussions that have nothing to do with real life.

➢ This is also the "Counseling" gift. People who have it enjoy spending hours helping other people work through their problems.

➢ It is also the "Cheerleading" gift. People who have it love to shout encouragement to those on the field—"You can do it. We're behind you all the way. Don't quit now." Encouragers are often good leaders, but they don't feel like they have to lead. They are just as happy to cheer on someone else.

Thank God for the men and women who encourage the rest of us. What a sad and dreary world it would be without them. They light the way and lift us up when we fall down. Many of us would have quit long ago if someone hadn't encouraged us to keep on going. In my book entitled, **"Total Surrender, Walking by Faith,"** I tell the story of my fourth grade teacher telling me "that I would never amount to anything in life." These words followed me all through high school. Even after my wife and I were married, I never could seem to accomplish anything that would give me a good future. Failure was my "middle" name until my close family would often say, "Where are you working now?" Then the opportunity opened for me to train in an area of life that I had never been exposed to in much detail. If it were not for two men that encouraged me in training and as I continued in the job, before I surrendered to the ministry, I would have failed, but through their encouragement, I became successful as far as the secular world was concerned in my position. It was through their encouragement that I was able to know that God could use me in His ministry. So if you have this gift, just remember how important you are to someone like me and maybe even you before you became an encourager.

Well let's look at a wonderful exhibit in the Word of God of a dynamic, yet unknown encourager.

BARNABAS

I believe that in the entire Bible there is no greater example of this gift in action than Barnabas. He is the height of the gift of encouragement.

We find that the most of his story is told in the book of Acts. In fact, there are seven different occasions when he used this spiritual gift and proved himself to be a true "Son of Encouragement."

He Helped An Unpopular Convert:

In Acts chapter 9, we find the story of the conversion of Saul of Tarsus. It begins like this:

"¹And Saul, yet breathing out threatenings and slaughter against the disciples of the Lord, went unto the high priest,

²And desired of him letters to Damascus to the synagogues, that if he found any of this way, whether they were men or women, he might bring them bound unto Jerusalem.

³And as he journeyed, he came near Damascus: and suddenly there shined round about him a light from heaven:

CHAPTER SEVEN

⁴And he fell to the earth, and heard a voice saying unto him, Saul, Saul, why persecutest thou me?

⁵And he said, Who art thou, Lord? And the Lord said, I am Jesus whom thou persecutest: [it is] hard for thee to kick against the pricks.

⁶And he trembling and astonished said, Lord, what wilt thou have me to do? And the Lord [said] unto him, Arise, and go into the city, and it shall be told thee what thou must do."

This is the most amazing conversion in the history of the Christian church. In the beginning, Saul was determined to murder the followers of Jesus. By the end, he has become a missionary of the gospel of Christ. First he would kill them, then he became one of them, then his former friends wanted to kill him.

The next few verses detail how a reluctant Ananias began to disciple this new convert. He must have done a good job because verse 23 tells us that "After many days had gone by, the Jews set out to kill him." But Saul learned of their plan. Day and night they kept close watch on the city gates in order to kill him. But his followers (the Christians he had formerly sworn to kill) took him by night and lowered him in a basket through an opening in the wall. We read in Acts 9:23-25, where it says,

"²³And after that many days were fulfilled, the Jews took counsel to kill him:

²⁴But their laying await was known of Saul. And they watched the gates day and night to kill him.

²⁵Then the disciples took him by night, and let [him] down by the wall in a basket."

So we find that he leaves Damascus to return to Jerusalem. The last time he was there he rampaged through the city; he was guilty of dragging believers out of their homes and putting them in prison. Now he returns as a follower of the One that he had once tried to destroy.

There is a problem though. The Christians in Jerusalem know absolutely nothing about his conversion. They haven't heard a word about it. To them, this

Saul is still their enemy. They could not forget what he did and they had been praying he would never come back.

But he does for verse 26 tell us what happens then. ***"And when Saul was come to Jerusalem, he assayed to join himself to the disciples: but they were all afraid of him, and believed not that he was a disciple."*** Well who could blame them? After all, what better way to destroy the church than to fake a conversion, infiltrate the ranks, gain the trust of the leadership, and then put them all in the jail? It's exactly the kind of sneaky plan the old Saul would have dreamed up.

So they don't want anything to do with this so-called convert. He has a reputation. He has a "devilish" past. Not that long ago he was trying to kill them. Now he claims to be converted. Their desire was to just leave him alone and not get involved in any way with him.

When we think of Barnabas and all of his quite achievements, and how he was an encourager to Paul and young John Mark, we know that he was a great leader, but it was through his servanthood heart that made him a great leader.

Let's be reminded again of the definition of what is a Christian servanthood/ leader? Basically speaking, this person is more or less a Christian leader as that person exerts more or less Christian influence in Christian ways. Or to put it another way, ***to the degree that you shape others toward the image of Christ, you are a Christian leader.***

That's a very broad definition of Christian leadership, and should include every obedient Christian, because we should all be influencing someone to be more like Christ. But if we get more specific, what we usually mean by a good Christian leader is someone who is really good at influencing others toward the life of Christ. They have personal strengths that draw others into

CHAPTER SEVEN

the sway of their influence and lead them to the ways of Christ.

Leadership is the key . . . There is a worldwide lack of men and women truly called of God and deeply taught in the Scriptures to lead the churches—people willing to suffer scorn, poverty and the shame of the Cross of Christ for the sake of the Savior who redeemed them. Those who accurately and effectively expound the Scriptures are few, especially in areas where the churches are growing rapidly.

There are people who oppose leadership wherever it begins to emerge. But if we had time, I would love to test the following claim by the Scriptures: Opposition to Christian leadership (or an anti-leadership mentality) is not born out of great vision, but out of little resentments. It has been said, "A church without strong leaders is not a democracy of giants." This diagnosis is right, because it is biblical. What the church needs worldwide is Spirit-filled, Bible-saturated, Christ-exalting, self-abasing, untiring, persevering leaders who exert deep, broad, life-changing influence for Jesus Christ.

There is definitely the Need for Leader-Makers and to get them we need hundreds and thousands of Barnabas-like leader-makers. I am not talking mainly today about leaders. I am talking about leader-makers. Are you one? Could you be one? Don't rule yourself out too quickly.

Charles Spurgeon was the greatest preacher of the 19th century. Listen to what he says about Mary King, the housekeeper at the school he attended as a teenager in Newmarket: "She liked something very sweet indeed, good strong Calvinistic doctrine, but she lived strongly as well as fed strongly. Many a time we have gone over the covenant of grace together, and talked of the personal election of the saints, their union to Christ, their final perseverance and what vital godliness meant; and I do believe that I learned more from her than I should have learned from any six doctors of divinity of the sort we have nowadays."

GIVE ME AN OLD SHOE

The most important thing you may ever do for the cause of Christ may go unnoticed for 30 years. Don't quench the Spirit of God as you read this chapter, He may be calling you to be a leader-maker.

What is the definition of a Christian servanthood/leader?
_____
_____
_____

What is the "cheerleading gift?"
_____
_____
_____

Let's look now at the:

Five Marks of a Biblical Leader-Maker

What are the marks of a biblical leader-maker? That's today's question and will be until The Lord Jesus returns for His church. There are at least five that I see in the life of Barnabas.

Under the providence of God in the life of the early church, we owe the ministry of two leaders to the initiative and advocacy of Barnabas. The two leaders are Paul and John Mark. As far as we know, Barnabas wrote none of the New Testament. But the men he nurtured wrote a third of it: Paul wrote thirteen of the epistles of the New Testament and Mark wrote one of our four gospels.

CHAPTER SEVEN

Let's look at the marks of a biblical leader-maker in the life of Barnabas - the man whom the apostles nicknamed, "son of encouragement" (Acts 4:36).

1. Risk-Taking

A biblical leader-maker takes risks to support hopeful leaders.

Acts 9:26 says that some time after Saul's conversion he came to Jerusalem and tried to join the disciples. You remember he had previously persecuted Christians. He was the High Priest's hatchet man, you might say.

Now here he is claiming to be a Christian convert. The last part of Acts 9:26 says, "They were all afraid of him, and believed not, for they did not believe that he was a disciple."

Is there anyone who will take a risk for Saul? Is there anyone who can see in him the making of a great leader? One man came forward. One man stuck his neck out when everyone else was afraid to give Saul a chance to prove himself—Barnabas (Verse 27):

- **a)** Barnabas took him, and brought him to the apostles.

- **b)** Barnabas became his advocate and look at the result. The church accepted him and his ministry flourished in Jerusalem. And Barnabas watched, and made note. This would not be the last time he supported Paul's ministry.

So the first mark of a biblical leader-maker is the willingness to take risks on behalf of potential leaders. All the other disciples were afraid. But the leader-maker had the courage to give this remarkable young man Saul a chance. What a pay-off!

2. Having a Good Eye and a Glad Heart

A biblical leader-maker has a good eye and a glad heart for the potential of grace.

Looking for the Embers of Grace

This is a recap of one of the points from Acts 11:23. When the church in Jerusalem heard that a church had been planted in Antioch, the one man that they thought would be a good encourager for the new Gentile believers was Barnabas. Barnabas could always find something good to encourage in people!

So Acts 11:23 says, "When he came and had seen the grace of God, he was glad." He had a good eye and a glad heart for the potential of grace. The church was new and imperfect, but Barnabas saw the work of grace and it made him glad. That is the mark of a leader-maker, or a "son of encouragement," as the apostles called him.

Leader-makers have their heat sensors adjusted and alert for embers of grace that they can fan, while the other kind of people, it seems, have their buckets of criticism ready to pour on the ashes of imperfection. So a leader-maker has a good eye and a glad heart for the potential of grace.

The Example of One of Our Missionaries

One of the most gifted persons in this regard that served on our church staff until his leaving for Ethiopia is Craig Dyson, one of our missionaries. I marvel as I speak to him and read his letters from the field, and how he and his wife Amanda speak of all unbelievers who are so close to trusting Christ. They see signs, by faith, of hope in almost everyone.

The Dyson's seem to have that determined, crisis mentality that sees people as fixed in their separation from God and stationary until some crisis crashes in and converts them. Instead they have such a view that sees people, to be sure, as really cut off from God and in need of conversion, but not as static. People are in motion spiritually. God is at work in a hundred ways to influence them, and they have an positive glowing heart for these signs of grace.

> *"A leader-maker has a good eye and a glad heart for the potential of grace."*

3. Humble and Self-Effacing

Biblical leader-makers are humble and self-effacing.

That means that they have the beautiful gift of fading into the background while pushing others into prominence. They are not addicted to the praise of men and do not crave the limelight.

What He Does When His Ministry Flourishes

Where do we see this in Barnabas? It starts in Acts 11:25–26. Barnabas' ministry in Antioch had been so successful that the converts were everywhere.

Now there is one kind of person who would say at this point: "I am now a respected leader. I have earned a good reputation for my work. It is now time to consolidate my gains and establish myself as a prominent preacher in this part of Syria."

But what does Barnabas do? Instead of maneuvering for his own exaltation, he leaves town to look for an associate—an associate that he knows good and well is a more dynamic leader and a better preacher than he is, namely, Saul.

So Barnabas went to Tarsus to look for Saul; and when he had found him, he brought him to Antioch. For a whole year they met with the church, and taught a large company of people.

With this personal investment in Saul's life and career, Barnabas secured forever his secondary status in church history—and don't you just love him for it?

What Does Barnabas Do When He Fades into Paul's Shadow?

Watch what happens as Barnabas fades into Paul's shadow, like an aircraft mechanic fades into the shadow of the soaring pilot.

In Acts 13:1–3 the Holy Spirit sets Barnabas and Saul apart for a missionary journey to the unreached cities of Cyprus and Galatia. Notice the order of the names in Acts 13:2 - it is still Barnabas first and Saul second, the way it was back in Acts 11:30 and 12:25.

When they get to the city of Paphos on the island of Cyprus, the proconsul invites them to speak to him, and in Acts 13:7, Barnabas still has the honor of first place: "he summoned Barnabas and Saul and sought to hear the word of God."

CHAPTER SEVEN

But when Elymas the magician tried to turn the proconsul away from the faith, it was Saul who exploded with the Holy Spirit in Acts 13:10: "*thou child of the devil, thou enemy pervert the right ways of the Lord?*"

This is probably not the way Barnabas would have said it. But from this point on, Saul (now called Paul for the first time in Acts 13:9) is in charge.

We see this immediately in Acts 13:13. Luke says, "Now Paul and his company set sail from Paphos." Barnabas is not even mentioned. In Acts 13:16 it is Paul not Barnabas who delivers the sermon in Antioch of Pisidia. When both of them are mentioned, it is now "Paul and Barnabas" not "Barnabas and Paul" (13:43, 46, 50; 15:2, 22, 35; except in Jerusalem where Barnabas is on his home turf, 15:12, 25; and in Lystra where Barnabas is called Zeus, and Paul, Hermes).

In Acts 14 we get a glimpse of what their partnership looked like. They have come to Lystra and a man has been healed through the hand of Paul. In Acts 14:11-12, look at how the local people describe the relationship between Barnabas and Paul:

> When the crowds saw what Paul had done, they lifted up their voices, saying in Lycaonian, "The gods have come down to us in the likeness of men!" Barnabas they called Zeus, and Paul, because he was the chief speaker, they called Hermes.
>
> Zeus of course is the father of the Greek gods. His Roman name is Jupiter. And Hermes is his son and is the fleet footed messenger of the gods. His Roman name is Mercury.

So Barnabas is perceived as older and more venerable and dignified than Paul. But Paul is the one who speaks with amazing force. Barnabas keeps a consistent strategy: put this young leader forward. Let him have the word.

GIVE ME AN OLD SHOE

Two Roles and Two Costs

And so behind the emergence of the greatest missionary and the greatest theologian is the aging Barnabas, humbly giving way to the explosive young leader named Paul. Sons of encouragement are less likely to be stoned than sons of thunder.

These two roles have their different costs. Barnabas pays the price of self-effacement and eventual obscurity. Paul pays the price here in Lystra of being stoned. Acts 14:19 describes how Paul, not Barnabas, bears the wrath of the cities.

What does it mean for the Biblical leader-makers to be humble and self-effacing?

_____
_____
_____
_____

A biblical leader-maker is humble and self-effacing. He looks for people with better gifts than his own and pushes them forward.

4. Patient with the Failure of Others

A biblical leader-maker is patient with the failures of others.

This will be clear from the way Barnabas handles the desertion of John Mark.

5. Free from Materialism

A biblical leader-maker is free from materialism.

CHAPTER SEVEN

He Doesn't Love Money, He Loves People.

In Acts 4:36, we find that Luke tells us that the apostles gave Joseph the name Barnabas because it meant "son of encouragement." The very next verse says, "He sold a field which belonged to him, and brought the money and laid it at the apostles' feet." Why did he do this? Acts 4:34-35 says that it was to meet the needs of the poor in the Christian community. This is what Luke associates with Barnabas' being a "son of encouragement."

> "Have we not power to eat and to drink? Have we not power to lead about a sister, a wife, as well as other apostles, and as the brethren of the Lord, and Cephas? Or I only and Barnabas, have not we power to forbear working?" (1 Corinthians 9:4–6).

Twenty years have passed and here is the old "Zeus and the younger Hermes" keeping themselves lean for the Lord, working with their hands, refusing to take gifts from Corinth. Why? They wanted to make it perfectly clear that they do not minister for money. They minister for people.

What Biblical Leader-Makers Dream Of

If you want to be a biblical leader-maker, ask yourself this: when my mind is free to dream, do I dream of clothes or cars or houses or lake property or sports or profits or stereos or videos or computers or vacations or food or movies or investments . . . ? In other words, am I materialistic in the moments when I dream about what I would like to do and to have? Does my mind naturally fill up with possessions?

That is not what fills the mind of a biblical leader-maker.

GIVE ME AN OLD SHOE

When leader-makers lie awake at night, their minds turn to people—people potentials and people strategies. They dream about how to maximize their influence on people for the sake of Christ. Think about these opportunities:

- I could invite that eleven year old boy or girl to attend our youth program at our church.

- We could get behind that missionary program by giving my financial support, or our local neighborhood ministry.

- We could ask that student over for Thanksgiving dinner . . .

- We could give an anonymous gift to that struggling seminary student . . .

- I could send him a note of thanks for that pastoral prayer . . .

- I could read my children a series of missionary stories . . .

- I could write that short-termer a letter of encouragement . . .

The list is endless for biblical leader-makers—people who are free from the heart-deadening mentality of materialism.

Summary

Well, there is Barnabas, the maker of a great leader.

- He took a risk to support a dangerous new convert.

- He had a good eye and a glad heart for the potential of grace.

CHAPTER SEVEN

- ➤ He was humble and self-effacing and let himself fade behind the rising star of the apostle Paul.

- ➤ He was patient with the failures of others.

- ➤ He was free from materialism and filled with thoughts and dreams of how to make leaders for the Lord of glory.

May the Lord fill His church with leader-makers for the cause of Christ here and around the world.

LET'S REVIEW:

Define *parakaleo:*

_____
_____
_____

What does a biblical leader-maker, who is humble and self-effacing, look for in people with better gifts?

_____
_____
_____
_____

> *"A biblical leader-maker is patient with the failures of others."*

~ 8 ~

~ Servanthood ~

"LIVING IT OUT"

GIVE ME AN OLD SHOE

ୡ

*S*ome time ago I read this expression from an old author: ***"The first duty of a clergyman is humbly to ask of God that all that he wants done in his hearers should first be truly and fully done in himself."*** These words are powerful words and certainly could be added to the servant/leader as well as the preacher. What a solemn application this is to the subject that occupied our attention in previous chapters--the living and working under the fullness of the Holy Spirit! And yet, if we understand our calling aright, our area of service according to our spiritual gifts, every one of us will have to say, "That is the one thing on which everything depends." What good is it to teach and lead men that they may be filled with the Spirit of God, if, when they ask us, "Has God done it for you?"

Look at the Lord Jesus Christ; when He had received the Holy Ghost from heaven, that John the Baptist said that "He would baptize with the Holy Ghost." As a server of the Lord Jesus Christ, I can only teach others what God has given to me. If my life as a servant be a life in which the flesh still greatly

CHAPTER EIGHT

prevails, if my life be a life in which I grieve the Holy Spirit of God, I cannot expect but that those that have listened to me preach or teach, will receive through me a very mingled kind of life. But if the life of God dwells in me, and if I am filled with His power, then I can hope and trust that the life that goes out from me may be infused into those that have heard me.

In each chapter of this book I have tried to touch on the need of every servant being filled with the Spirit; and what is there of deeper interest to us now, or that can better occupy our attention, than prayerfully to consider how we can bring to those that believe that this is possible; and how we can lead on every believer to seek it for himself, to expect it, and to accept it, so as to live it out? The message must come from us as a witness of our personal experience, by the grace of God.

When we look at the importance of the leadership of the Holy Spirit in our lives, we must take the examples given to us in the Word of God. For example, in the gospel by John, we read that John the Baptist was told that upon whom he would see the Spirit descending and abiding, He it was who would baptize with the Spirit. Thus John the Baptist led the people on from Christ to the expectation of the Holy Ghost for themselves. And what did Jesus do? For three years, He was with His disciples, teaching and instructing them; but when He was about to go away, in His farewell discourse on the last night, what was His great promise to the disciples? "I will pray the Father, and He shall give you another Comforter, even the Spirit of truth." Christ's constant work was to teach His disciples to expect the Holy Spirit.

It was the Holy Ghost who was given to the church at Pentecost; and it is the Holy Ghost who gives Pentecostal blessings today. It is this power, given to bless men, that wrought such wonderful lives, love, and self-sacrifice in the early church; and it is this that makes us look back to those days as the most beautiful part of the Church's history. And it is the same Spirit of power that must dwell in the hearts of all believers in our day to give the Church its true position and leadership and servanthood. It is therefore that every minister and Christian worker be endued with the power of the Holy Ghost; that He may search us and try us, and enable us sincerely to answer the question, "Have I known the indwelling and the filling of the Holy Spirit that God wants me to have as I serve Him?"

Let me quote R. A. Torrey. *"Now, if we are indeed to come into full harmony with these two great principles, then there come to us some further questions of the very deepest importance. And the first question is: -- Why is it that there is in the church of Christ so little practical acknowledgment of the power of the Holy Ghost? I am not speaking to you, brethren, as if I thought you were not sound in doctrine on this point. I speak to you as believing in the Holy Ghost as the third person in the ever-blessed Trinity. But I speak to you confidently as to those who will readily admit that the truth or the presence and of the power of the Holy Ghost is not acknowledged in the church as it ought to be. Then the question is, "Why is it not so acknowledged? I answer because of its spirituality. It is one of the most difficult truths in the Bible for the human mind to comprehend. God has revealed Himself in creation throughout the whole universe. He has revealed Himself in Christ incarnate--and what a subject of study the person, and word, and works of Christ form! But the mysterious indwelling of the Holy Spirit, hidden in the depths of the life of the believer, how much less easy to comprehend!"*

In the early Pentecostal days of the church, this knowledge was intuitive; they *possessed* the Spirit in power. But soon after the spirit of the world began to creep into the church and mastered it. This was followed by the deeper darkness of formality and superstition in the Roman Catholic Church, when the spirit of the world completely triumphed in what was

CHAPTER EIGHT

improperly styled the Church of Christ. The Reformation in the days of Luther restored the truth of justification by faith in Christ; but the doctrine of the Holy Ghost did not then obtain its proper place, for God does not reveal all truth at one time.

A great deal of the spirit of the world was still left in the reformed churches; but now God is awakening the church to strive after a fuller scriptural idea of the Holy Spirit's place and power.

Through the medium of books, Bible conferences, Bible preaching, and conventions, many hearts are being stirred.

When I first started in the secular world, the word ***Leadership*** was emphasized greatly to move up the line in the company and a qualification to become a leader. When I entered the ministry, and in Bible school, this also was emphasized to us that were called to be pastors and the importance of being a leader. When we think of the church in America, what exactly is meant by real leadership? Many books and resources are available on this subject, and to be honest, most of them are fluff and nonsense, and ignore the truths of God's Word! I have spent most of my ministerial career or forty-three years studying leadership to be a better pastor and teacher. The qualities are found in the Person; work and life of our Lord Jesus Christ is the best teacher of what a leader is to be, or should I say, Servant.

We usually know what the world calls us to, but do you know what God calls you to? As we study the Bible, we find that we are called, the saved, to a higher level of excellence one of vision, love, integrity, and functionality. As our name **Christian** gives meaning, we are to be Christ-like, not in the realm of the world. We are to be influencers but not partakers, and our modes of leading the church must ***follow suit.*** Servanthood is about caring for people because we are being dependent upon Him and His precepts in order to be real and effectual in Kingdom values and the modeling of His ways to the world (Philippians 2:6-8).

Servanthood and who you are, is found in the life of our Lord Jesus Christ, as "He took a towel" and I keep on emphasizing John 13:2-5, as our greatest example. Jesus is teaching us through His example that this kind of leadership produces a church filled with real purpose and motivation as people are called, appreciated, loved, encouraged, involved by mentoring and being a part of the discipleship program before they are deployed in ministry. This is "Christ life" before "ministry life." Thus, the leadership of Christ is producing a church of spiritual maturity and involvement so that the people are inspired to be surrendered as in caught up in Christ and with one another to be more admirable in the faith and in the world making Him known. This kind of servanthood sees Christ and we become imitators of Christ.

Who we are as Christians needs to transcend in how we react to one another. Servanthood that is effective, even in the business world, is more about how we treat and empower our workers and staff. I like this statement that I once read, "When we are with Christ, we are with one another, and we *bear with one another in love.*" Servanthood is about being humble-minded, gentle, and patient; it is about our lives being truly rooted and grounded in Christ so our focus is to glorify Him rather than follow trends or lift ourselves up. It requires us to be deeper, lasting, and real in Christ so our model of servanthood then focuses on Christ and not us. It causes people to see Christ at work in us.

Servanthood is never about pride or leading others to us and ignoring Christ. If so, it is not biblical nor is it being a servant! We are to take Christ, and unselfishly make the best of our goods, resources, and situations to move the church of God in the direction He called us to.

CHAPTER EIGHT

Jesus clearly tells us that a servant should behave like a servant as we find in Luke 22:26. We are not to serve for power, control, or for personal gain. Rather, we are to point others in His direction by our example.

Again, let's look at how Jesus *took a towel* and washed His disciples' feet. This is an act we can easily glance over, missing its significance. But this was God, the Creator of the universe, performing the lowest job in that culture, washing someone's feet.

Real, biblical servanthood is never a force of will or personality. Servant hood embodies the fruit and character of our Lord. It requires your being a servant before you attempt to direct others. If a leader just directs and never serves, there is a good chance he is not a real leader; rather, he or she is a pretender, exercising his agenda and not God's call and will.

We are called to be Servants. It is how Christ led. He exemplifies it in how He cares for and gently guides us. He, as God, serves as our prime example, the One to whom we are responsible for the people He has entrusted to us. We can trust Christ to lead us, John10:11; 1 Peter 2:25 and thus lead others in the same manner.

Dear Christian, should not this be our desire today as in every day? It is our privilege to take part in this great privilege to preach, teach and serve in the work more earnestly than ever. Let each of us who have the privilege to teach God's Word and serve in His ministry, say my great work is to lead men to the saving knowledge of Christ as their Savior and then to grow in His Word.

In concluding this thought, dear Christian, if you and I am Christ's, we should take our places and claim our privilege. We are witnesses to the truth which we believe, witnesses to the reality of what Jesus does and what He is, by His presence in our own souls. If we are willing to be such servants for

GIVE ME AN OLD SHOE

Christ, let us go to our God, let us make confession and surrender, and by faith claim what God has for us as servants of the gospel and workers in His service. God will prove faithful. Even at this very moment, He will touch your hearts with a deep consciousness of His faithfulness and of His presence; and He will give to every hungering, trustful one that which we continually need.

Let me share with you as we conclude our thoughts on this chapter, the following by Charles Spurgeon, the great preacher and pastor of England, on this subject.

Matthew 26:7-9 says, "There came unto him a woman having an alabaster box of very precious ointment, and poured it on his head, as he sat *at* meat. But when his disciples saw *it*, they had indignation, saying, To what purpose *is* this waste? For this ointment might have been sold for much, and given to the poor."

Read Matthew 26:10-13. Being aware of this, Jesus said to them, "Why trouble ye the woman? For she hath wrought a good work upon me. For ye have the poor always with you; but me ye have not always. For in that she hath poured this ointment on my body, she did *it* for my burial. Verily I say unto you, Wheresoever this gospel shall be preached in the whole world, *there* shall also this, that this woman hath done, be told for a memorial of her."

Study carefully the story of the enthusiastic Christian woman who poured the alabaster jar of very precious perfume on the head of our blessed Lord and Savior. Her first and last thoughts were for the Lord Jesus Himself.

Seek to do something for Jesus, which will be above all, a secret sacrifice of pure love to Jesus. Do special and secretive work towards your Lord. Between you and your Lord let there be secret tokens of love. You will say to me, "What shall I do?" I cannot answer for I am not to be a judge for

CHAPTER EIGHT

you; especially as to a private deed of love. The good woman did not say to Peter, "What shall I give?" nor to John, "What shall I do?" but her heart was imaginative. I will only say, that we might offer more private prayer for the Lord Jesus. "Pray for Him and bless Him all day long," (Psalm 72:15). Intercede for your neighbors; pray for yourselves; but could you set apart a little time each day in which prayer should be all for Jesus?

Could you at such times cry with secret pleadings, "Hallowed be your name! Your kingdom come! Your will be done on earth, as it is in heaven?" Wouldn't it be a sweet thing to feel at such a time -- I shall now go to my bedroom, and give my Lord a few minutes of my heart's warmest prayer, that He may see the concern of my soul for Him? That is one thing which all saints can do.

Another holy offering is adoration -- the adoring of Jesus. Don't we all too often forget this adoration in our churches and shove it into a corner? The best part of all of our church services is the worship -- the direct worship; and in this, the first place should be given to the worship of the Lord Jesus. We sing at times to edify one another with psalms and spiritual songs, but we should also sing simply and only to glorify Jesus. We are to do this publicly in corporate worship; but shouldn't we also do it alone? Shouldn't we all, if we can, find a period in which we will spend the time, not in seeking the good of our fellow-men, not in seeking our own good, but in adoring Jesus, blessing Him, magnifying Him, praising Him, pouring out our heart's love towards Him and presenting our soul's reverence and concern. I suggest this to you. I can't teach you how to do it. God's Holy Spirit must show your hearts the way.

I offer you one or two suggestions about doing good works for Jesus.

First, take care that self never creeps in. It is to be all for Jesus: don't let the dirty fingers of self-seeking stain your work. Never do anything for

Jesus out of the love for popularity. Be always glad if your right hand does not know what your left hand does. Hide your works as much as possible from the praise of your closest friend. At the sametime, let me also add; never have any fear of rejection from those who don't understand your love for Jesus.

This good woman did her work publicly, because it was the best way to honor her Lord; and if you can honor Him by doing a good work publicly before all men, then do not be afraid. To some, the temptation may be to catch the public eye; to others, the temptation may be to dread it. Serve your Lord as if no eye sees you; but do not blush if all the eyes in the universe should gaze upon you. Don't let self, in either case, come in to defile the service.

Secondly, Never congratulate yourself after you have done a work for Jesus. If you say to yourself, "Well done!" you have sacrificed to yourself. Try to always feel that if you had done all that should have been done; it would only have been your reasonable service. Remember that deeds of self-sacrifice are most acceptable to Jesus. He loves His people's gifts when they give, and feel that they have given. We should measure what we do for Him not by what we have given, but by what we have left; and if we have a lot left over then we haven't given as much as the widow who gave two very small copper coins--no, for certain we have not, for she gave "all she had to live on."

Let us, above all, keep out of our heart the thought which is so common in this life that nothing is worth doing unless something practical comes out of it -- meaning by "practical" some obvious consequence on the morals of others. Almost everyone asks the question, "What good will it do? What good will it do for me? What good will it do for my neighbor? What is the purpose of this effort?" No, the real issue is, if it will glorify Christ, do it; and accept that motive as the highest and most conclusive of reasons.

CHAPTER EIGHT

If a deed done for Christ causes you to be disliked, and threatens to deprive you of usefulness, then do it anyway. I count my own character, popularity, and usefulness to be nothing compared with the devotion to the Lord Jesus. It is the devil's logic which says, "You see I can't share the truth, because I am afraid of the consequences." What have we to do with consequences? Be honest, and fear not! The consequences are God's concerns, and not yours. If you have done a good work for Christ, though to you it may appear that it has caused a lot of problems, yet you have already done it, then Christ has accepted it, and He will make a note of it, and in your conscience He will smile to you His approval.

There is a good defense for any kind of work which you may do for Jesus and for Jesus only. However great the cost, nothing is wasted which is spent on the Lord, for Jesus deserves it. What if it did nothing for others; did it please Him? He has a right to it. Is nothing to be done for the Master of the feast? Are we to be looking after the sheep so much that we never honor the shepherd? Are the Lord's servants to be cared for while we do nothing for the Precious Lord Himself? I have sometimes felt in my soul the wish that I had no one to serve but my Lord. When I have tried to do my best to serve God, and a heartless critic has torn my work to pieces, I have thought, "I didn't do it for you! I wouldn't have done it for you! I did it for my Lord. Your judgment is a small matter. You condemn my zeal for the truth. You condemn what He commands."

Thus you may go about your service, and feel "I do it for Christ, and I believe that Christ accepts my service, and I am content with that." Jesus deserves that much should be done for Him. Do you doubt that? A birthday present is given to dad on his birthday. That present is of no use to mom, or to the children; it cannot be eaten, it cannot be worn; dad could not give it away to anybody, it is of no value to anybody but himself. Does anybody say, "What a pity such a gift was selected, even though dad is pleased?" No, everybody says, "That is just the thing we like to give to dad, since it is something he needs personally. We meant it to be for him; we felt this was the perfect gift for him, and we are glad that the gift will bring him pleasure."

As you serve Christ, find out what will please Him; and do it for Him. Think of no one else in the matter. He deserves all you can do for Him, and infinitely more. Besides, you may be sure that any action which appears to you as useless, if prompted by love, has a place in Christ's plan, and will be turned into something of great value. This anointing of our Lord's head was said to be useless. "No," said Jesus, "When she poured this perfume on my body, she did it to prepare me for burial." There have been men who have done a heroic deed for Christ, and at the time they did it they might have asked, "How will this serve my Lord's purpose?" But somehow it was the very thing that was wanted. When the great preachers Whitefield and Wesley went out into the open fields to preach, it was thought to be a fanatical innovation, and perhaps they, themselves, would not have ventured upon it if there had not been an absolute necessity; but what seemed to that age a daring deed, set an example to all of England, and open-air preaching has become an accepted agency of great worth. If you, for Christ's sake, become visionary, don't worry, your folly may be the wisdom of the ages to come.

The woman's loving act was not wasted; for it has helped us all down to this very moment. There has it stood in the Bible; and all who have read it, and are right in their heart, have been motivated by it to sacred consecration out of love to Jesus. That woman has been a preacher to nineteen centuries; the influence of that alabaster jar is not exhausted today, and never will be. Whenever you meet a friend in Europe, Asia, Africa, or America, who has done anything for our Lord Jesus, you still smell the perfume of the sacred spikenard. Her act is doing all of us good at this hour; it is filling this church with fragrance.

CHAPTER EIGHT

If you are serving Christ in your own secret way in which you do not seek to benefit others, but to honor Him, it may be you will be an instructive example to saints in ages to come. Oh, that I could stir some hearts to personal consecration to Jesus, my Lord! Young men and women, we want missionaries to go abroad.

We need young preachers that will stand firm on the Word of God and preach His Word without apology or compromise.

What about you dear layperson? Are you willing to become that servant that God has called you many years ago and you have yet to surrender? Why not now?

Search your heart right now before going on to the next chapter.

Read John11:7-18 and in your own words where does your life fit in and what area of God's work is He calling you.

_____

_____

_____

_____

_____

s

9

~ Servanthood ~

"THE SECRET OF SERVING"

CHAPTER NINE

In this chapter we will walk through servanthood by looking in John chapter twenty-one where it has been considered a dynamic scene for Christ and His disciples and probably at the most popular body of water that most love to visit when in the Holy land, the Sea of Galilee. With this thought in mind, let's look at the participants, that Dr. J. Vernon McGee called, ***"the convention of problem children, each with a problem of his own."***

First, let's look at Simon Peter. Here is the impulsive, affectionate and impetuous Peter.

Second, there was Thomas, Thomas the skeptic, always raising some question or even casting doubt.

Thirdly, we find Nathanael, known as a doubter at the beginning of the ministry of Christ. If you recall, he was the one that made the statement, "Can anything good come out of Nazareth?"

GIVE ME AN OLD SHOE

Fourth we see a group of brothers, James and John, who Jesus named, "the sons of thunder."

Finally, we are told there were two other, but they were not named; maybe we can identify them as you and me, *the other problem children*.

So, now the rest of the story, where we find these men waiting for Jesus as He commanded them, Matthew 28:10. As most of us are, their patience ran out and Peter of course, said, "I am going fishing," and so the other six went with him and to their surprise, not one fish was caught.

There is a lesson here to be learned, even though they were professionals at fishing, that was their livelihood before they started following Christ, but on that night was a failure because this was not the will of God for them, they were to "wait on Christ."

We are told in Psalms 1:3, that, "the man or woman, shall be like a tree planted by the rivers of water, *brings forth its fruit in its season."* A great preacher of God's Word said of this verse, *"the fruitage of man's labor will come forth at a time when it will fit into God's plan and purpose."* The problem that we are living in today in the churches, are that we are measuring success by numbers in attendance or programs that we have. When will we ever learn that spiritual values cannot be determined by figures and numbers of programs?

Notice in John 21:5, that Jesus asked them if they had anything to eat and notice their answer. "No," one quick short answer. You know, it is amazing how they answered Jesus' question, but did not want to continue the conversation.

As we think about servanthood, can you hear Jesus now saying to you and me, "have you caught anything?" I am convinced that the whole thought

CHAPTER NINE

that Jesus had here was that He is to direct our lives with directions and they are to be obeyed. When we fish according to His plans, there will be a bountiful supply.

We find after a good meal that Jesus supplied, there was conversation led by Jesus when He asked Peter if he loved Him, now notice He asked Peter three times; why three times? Could it be that Peter had denied Christ publicly three times and three times he makes an affirmation? We do know this, that this is the restoration of Peter to service.

I find it very interesting that after that night, Peter was through boasting of who and what he was and also that Jesus did not rebuke Peter for failure to rise to the heights of love, He recommissioned him and gave him his first assignment, "Feed my sheep" better yet, "Feed my lambs," the new Christians. Dear Christian, if you and I really love the Lord Jesus Christ, we will want to feed His lambs. Thank God every Sunday and during the week there are those that are feeding the lambs, but we need more and more feeding the Word of God to new converts. Then in the next moment, Jesus says to Peter, Shepherd My sheep." This simply means to discipline by giving them direction. I think we kind of have it mixed up today. We try to discipline the new Christians and feed the older ones, when Jesus meant to "feed the young ones and disciple the older ones."

What we need in the church today is a baptism of emotion, *a real genuine breaking of the heart and flowing of tears* that says, "Lord Jesus, You know that I love You!" It is time for the church and I mean, the Christian, let me go further, the Born again folks, to **"fall in Love with Jesus Christ!"**

What then is the secret of serving? Let me answer it by sharing this story. A great Bible teacher once said, that how a friend of his one night while the moon was raising, said, "He made that!" Then that friend said something else. He said that every night before going to bed, he told the Lord Jesus, "I Love You."

GIVE ME AN OLD SHOE

That is the secret of serving and having a life and a ministry that your and my Lord can and will use. Why not try it?

Will you make that commitment right now? Then why not sign below and date it for a daily reminder that we are servants of the King of Kings and Lord of Lords.

Name: _____

Date: _____

We continue with Matthew 26:7-13, where we find a woman came to Jesus with an alabaster jar of very expensive perfume, which she poured on his head as he was reclining at the table. When the disciples saw this, they were indignant. "Why this waste?" they asked. "This perfume could have been sold at a high price and the money given to the poor."

As we think about the sacrifice she made for the Lord, we need to ask ourselves the question: Have we? Have we done what we could for Him? Have we given all there is to give? Notice three things she did what she could. As we do, search your heart and see if you have.

She Sacrificed

A pence was the daily wage of the average worker. Therefore, in modern terms, it was worth about $15.00. This spikenard was produced from a rare plant that grew in India. It was very expensive and many people saved for years to be able to provide this for their own funeral preparations.

CHAPTER NINE

Two ancient eastern customs are in here. The first has to do with the breaking of glasses. When a distinguished person ate in a home, often the glass they had used was broken to prevent a lesser person from using it in the future. This may have been in this lady's mind as she broken the box. Another custom had to do with burial rituals. After the body of the deceased had been washed and anointed, the box that had contained the embalming spices was broken and the fragments were buried with the individual. I like to imagine that she broke the vessel so that she might extract every drop of ointment for use on the Lord Jesus.

So, regardless of the reason, one thing is clear: This dear lady gave all she had to Jesus for His glory! I wonder have we broken the alabaster box of our life and poured out ourselves, every drop for Him.

As a Christian, we should look at our lives and ask ourselves if we have given everything we have and are to Him. You see, sacrifice was the ultimate expression of love and worship of the Lord Jesus. She gave all she had! Without going any further in this book, ask yourself this question, have I placed everything on the altar for Him? Think about it seriously. What have you given to Him and what have you held back for yourself or for another?

She Served

Jesus said that she had done everything that was in her power. The expression "what she could" refers to all she possessed. There were many things she could not do for Jesus, but in anointing Him with that box of costly ointment, she was giving Him all she had. Her service was absolute. The implication for us is clear that when the Holy Spirit of God speaks to our hearts, that is the time to step up and serve God and quit wasting time. Too often, we miss out on those special moments of service to Jesus when we ignore the impulses and leadership of the Holy

Spirit. That is why the warning to be careful lest we "quench the Spirit of God," (1 Thessalonians 5:19).

She Surrendered

By kneeling to Christ and anointing Him, she was declaring her faith in Him as the Messiah. She was telling everyone who saw her do what she did that her faith was in the Lord Jesus Christ. She, at that moment, surrendered all to Him!

It certainly seems that Mary, finally I have told you who this woman was. She was more in touch with Who Jesus was than were His own disciples. She believed that He was about to die. They did not! Apparently she knew that His body would not be available to anoint after death, so she did it ahead of time. No doubt her faith enabled her to see beyond the cross and the tomb to a day when Jesus would rise from the dead and occupy the throne of glory in Heaven. She was absolutely surrendered to the Lord Jesus Christ.

Friend, what about you? Are you surrendered to the same level as Mary? Does the life that you now live show you kneeling before Him as absolute Lord and God? Have you gotten to this place in your life that you have done all that you can do? At that point in your spiritual walk, He will be everything and we will be nothing. The servant leader will find yourselves lost in His glory. The question is are you there yet, or are there pieces of your life that remain not surrendered? It is time for the Christian to break our lives on His altar so that *"He might extract the very last drop of glory from us. That is the price of surrender!"*

There is a story from the Middle East of four brothers who decided to have a feast. As wine was rather expensive, they concluded that each should bring an equal quantity and add it to the common supply. However, one of

CHAPTER NINE

the brothers, thinking to escape the expense of such a contribution decided to bring water instead of wine. "It won't be noticed," he reasoned.

But at the feast when the wine was poured out it wasn't wine at all. It was only water. Each of the four brothers had thought alike, "Let the others do it. Water is less expensive."

This story can be told in many churches today where you'll find that everybody loves a servant but nobody wants to be one.

So with regard to Jesus, find out what will please Him; and do it for Him. Think of no one else in the matter. He deserves all you can do for Him, and infinitely more.

Besides, you may be sure that any action which appears to you as useless, if prompted by love, has a place in Christ's plan, and will be turned into something of great value.

What areas of service in Christ's ministry are you serving and why?

_____
_____
_____
_____
_____
_____
_____
_____
_____
_____
_____
_____

> ***It is time for the Christian to break our lives on His altar so that "He might extract the very last drop of glory from us. That is the price of surrender!"***

As a servant of Christ, there is a very special verse that has been drawn to my attention. Listen to this verse: ***"Ye are my friends, if ye do whatsoever I command you."*** (John 15:14).

It is a fact, the most inspiring words in the lexicon of language is the word, "friend." It is so true that when one has friends, he is rich in deed.

There are many accolades' that is given to men on earth and I am very humbled when someone introduces me as "their friend." Jesus applies this word "friend" to His own people and followers. I do not know of any other honor on this earth than to be called the "friend of Jesus."

I see this verse as one that applies to the servant that gives themselves to Christ in serving and then having Jesus to call you friend. And one of the most wonderful truths about the word "friend" is that Jesus Christ is a friend of every soul and His death was for all.

CHAPTER NINE

As I address this question to you, "Am I a really a true friend of Christ?" There are three simple ways to find out.

1. Have you trusted Christ as your personal Savior? I am not talking about knowing about Christ, but has there ever been a time that you asked Jesus to forgive you of your sins and accepted Him as your personal Savior? Can you say with Paul the Apostle, "I know in whom I have believed and am persuaded that He is able to keep that which I have committed unto Him against that day."

2. If you are a real friend of Christ, then you love Him. I mean with all your heart, all your innermost being, to the point that you have and will yield, surrender, yourself to Him, without reserve, unconditional surrender, and bowing before Him in your heart?

It is a known fact that when love is absent in a marriage, it robs all the beauty and sacredness of that marriage.

If love is absent from the church, how dead that church must be. In fact Jesus said in Revelation 2:3, "And hast borne, and hast patience, and for my name's sake hast laboured, and hast not fainted," verse 4, "Nevertheless, I have somewhat against thee, because that hast left thy first love..." As I see what Jesus is saying here, it is that they had not departed completely from the love for God; their love no longer had the fervency, depth or meaning it once had. It was a cooling of heart which had overtaken them in their relationship to God, and this dear church erased their Christian testimony! I believe there are seven reasons why Christians and churches lose their love and die:

a. Lack of leadership

b. Lack of vision for lost souls

c. Lack of spiritual maturity of the believers

d. Lack of prayer

e. Lack of Bible study

f. Lack of love for the saints

g. Lack of "death" to self

3. If you are truly a friend of Christ you will try to obey Him; you will desire to obey Him. You see, what Christ wants from you and me is friendship. Your friendship expressed in love, in obedience, in faith and affection. Do you have that friendship? The first question of one that has just been born again was asked of the apostle Paul after his visit from Jesus. Paul asked the question, "what wilt thou have me do?" As a Christian, you should not only ask this question of your Savior, but begin asking Him how He would want you to serve Him.

CHAPTER NINE

*If you are a real friend of Christ,
then you love Him.
I mean with all your heart,
all your innermost being,
to the point that you have and will yield,
surrender yourself to Him without reserve,
unconditional surrender,
and bowing before Him in your heart?*

10

~ Servanthood ~

"THE COST"

CHAPTER TEN

❦

We have seen the purpose of servanthood and many examples in God's Word about servanthood, and I know of no better passage of Scripture to conclude this book than what we find in John 15:20-16:4;

[20]"*Remember the word that I said unto you, The servant is not greater than his lord. If they have persecuted me, they will also persecute you; if they have kept my saying, they will keep yours also.*

[21]*But all these things will they do unto you for my name's sake, because they know not him that sent me.*

[22]*If I had not come and spoken unto them, they had not had sin: but now they have no clake for their sin.*

[23]*He that hateth me hateth my Father also.*

[24]*If I had not done among them the works which none other man did, they had not had sin: but now have they both seen and hated both me and my Father.*

[25]*But this cometh to pass, that the word might be fulfilled that is written in their law, They hated me without a cause.*

²⁶But when the Comforter is come, whom I will send unto you from the Father, even the Spirit of truth, which proceedeth from the Father, he shall testify of me:

²⁷And ye also shall bear witness, because ye have been with me from the beginning.

¹These things have I spoken unto you, that ye should not be offended.

²They shall put you out of the synagogues: yea, the time cometh, that whosoever killeth you will think that he doeth God service.

³And these things will they do unto you, because they have not known the Father, nor me.

⁴But these things have I told you, that when the time shall come, ye may remember that I told you of them. And these things I said not unto you at the beginning, because I was with you."

The world does not hate us because we are so holy. They hate us because of that image of Christ reflecting from us.

In this passage of Scripture, Jesus is telling His disciples why men and the world would not listen to their message of Christ and need of their following Him and they, the followers of Christ, would suffer even to the point of persecution and death. This truth can be seen all around our world and nation today as never before. Corruption is seen everywhere. Sin is on the rampage in such openness as never in the world before. We see the rise of abortion, killing on the streets, in our schools, public places of worship, entertainment and business establishments. The reason is simple; people do not know God or Christ and the pure gospel is not being preached from the pulpits of America. We are told by Jesus Himself that there would be in the last days, 2 Timothy 3:1-7, *"This know also, that in the last days perilous times shall come. ² For men shall be lovers of their own selves, covetous, boasters, proud, blasphemers, disobedient to parents, unthankful, unholy, ³ Without natu-*

CHAPTER TEN

ral affection, trucebreakers, false accusers, incontinent, fierce, despisers of those that are good, ⁴ Traitors, heady, highminded, lovers of pleasures more than lovers of God; ⁵ Having a form of godliness, but denying the power thereof: from such turn away. ⁶ For of this sort are they which creep into houses, and lead captive silly women laden with sins, led away with divers lusts, ⁷ Ever learning, and never able to come to the knowledge of the truth."

If we are to be the servants we are to be, according to the Word of God and given the examples in Scripture, the following will take place in our lives.

If you are a Christian, you are a soldier. You are called to live as a soldier. You have a mission. You're not here for personal comfort, but to accomplish the mission your Commander-in-Chief gave to us.

Suppose you were driving down the road in your car, and all of a sudden, you came upon a sign that said this, "Warning: Danger Ahead!" What would you do? You might turn around or look for an alternate route. In the least, you would slow down and proceed with caution. Why do we have warning signs? Warning signs alert us to impending danger.

In these verses, Jesus warned His disciples that there was danger ahead, danger, not just for Him, for them, too.

But why did Jesus give us this warning sign? So we could flee, or look for an alternate route? No, then why? Let's look closer as we find out what Jesus meant. "All this I have told you **so that** you will not go astray. They will put you out of the synagogue; in fact, a time is coming when anyone who kills you will think he is offering a service to God. They will do such things because they have not known the Father or me. I have told you this, **so that** when the time comes you will remember that I warned you. I did not tell you this at first because I was with you" (John 16:1-4).

Notice the repetition. Twice Jesus said, "I have told you this," verses 1 and in verse 4, and twice He told them why, simply put, Jesus' words in John 16:1-4 serve two purposes for us, one is negative and one is positive. If you want to know how to live in enemy territory you need to take heed.

Jesus' words protect us from doing the wrong thing (vv. 1-3).

The scene was sober that night. Jesus had already told the Twelve many things. He told them about His upcoming death, that He would be betrayed by one of them and the denial by all of them, chapter 16, verse 32, and they hardly knew what to say.

Our text begins with Jesus saying, "All this I have told you so that you will not go astray." Which raises the question, "All what?" What had Jesus just told the disciples?

The overall context is the Upper Room Discourse of John 14-15, in which Jesus sought to, prepare His followers for His departure. The immediate context is the latter half of John 15. There Jesus told the Twelve, with the absence of Judas, that the world would hate them (v. 19), that His Spirit would come and help them (v. 26), and that they were to testify about Him (v. 27). "All this I have told you." I want you to listen to the very words Jesus had just said in John 15:18-27. Pay careful attention to the repeated use of the term "hate." "If the world **hates** you, keep in mind that it **hated** me first. If you belonged to the world, it would love you as its own. As it is, you do not belong to the world, but I have chosen you out of the world. That is why the world **hates** you. Remember the words I spoke to you: 'No servant is greater than his master.' If they persecuted me, they will persecute you also. If they obeyed my teaching, they will obey yours also. They will treat you this way because of my name, for they do not know the One who sent me. If I had not come and spoken to them, they would not be guilty of sin. Now, however, they

CHAPTER TEN

have no excuse for their sin. He who **hates** me **hates** my Father as well. If I had not done among them what no one else did, they would not be guilty of sin. But now they have seen these miracles, and yet they have **hated** both me and my Father. But this is to fulfill what is written in their Law: 'They **hated** me without reason.' When the Counselor comes, whom I will send to you from the Father, the Spirit of truth who goes out from the Father, he will testify about me. And you also must testify, for you have been with me from the beginning."

"The world is going to hate you," Jesus said, "just like it hated me." "After I leave, you can expect the hatred to turn against you."

So then, why did Jesus give them this dismal warning?

"All this I have told you **so that** you will not" do something. If we take Jesus' words to heart, they will protect us from doing the wrong thing.

Jesus speaks bluntly to us about three subjects in John 16:1-3.

1. We have a duty.

Just what is our duty? We see it in John 16:1. No doubt, the unspoken question on the disciples' minds must have been, "Jesus, why are you telling us these things, this terrible news about the world's hatred?" What was Jesus' answer? John 16:1, "So that you will not go astray." The KJV says, "So you won't be offended." What does that mean?

The Greek term is *skandalizo*. What English word do you hear in that? Scandal. We know all about scandals in our day, don't we? Scandals that involve religious leaders, scandals involving politicians, and professional athletes, and music stars. A scandal is the result of someone "messing" up; not living up to the standards of one in the public eye and respect of that public or in the case of the Christian, the Christian walk.

By definition, the word in verse 1 means "to put a trap in the way which would cause a person to stumble." It carries the idea of surprise.

A thief does not tell you when he is going to come and rob you, and when the local law enforcement follows leads to his crimes, they do not send word to the thief that they know of his next robbery, they surprise him.

Here's Jesus' point, "Disciples, danger is coming. The reason I'm telling you this is so that when it does, you won't be caught off guard." The same goes for us.

    a. *When hard times come, we must not be surprised.*

    b. *What's more, we must not get sidetracked.*

We mustn't turn away from the Lord and choose the course of least resistance. That's not an option. We have a duty. Our duty is to be loyal to Christ, to refuse to "go astray" and get "offended" when things don't go smoothly.

By the way, don't miss an important sidelight here. The servant is responsible to inform those that they serve that the Christian life is not a bed of roses. That's what Jesus did. When we disciple new believers, and become servants, we need to follow the Lord's example and warn them that opposition is inevitable. We must tell them, it's thrilling to be a Christian and to serve others but remember what Christ told Peter that Satan wants to sift you as wheat. We have a Duty.

2. We will face danger.

"They will put you out of the synagogue; in fact, a time is coming when anyone who kills you will think he is offering a service to God."

CHAPTER TEN

No, Jesus never said the Christian life would be easy. Just the opposite. He said, "Proceed with caution. There's danger ahead."

One of the great deceivers of the "health and wealth" gopel preachers of our day is this. They minimize the danger.

William Tyndale knew that his duty involved danger. Tyndale lived in the 16th century. His sole passion in life was to translate the Bible into the English language so even the common people could read it. He met great opposition from the religious leaders. He was severely persecuted, and eventually burned at the stake. In spite of all of this, here's what he said, "I never expected anything else." He expected to suffer for Jesus. Why are we surprised when we have to suffer for Christ?

Jesus said we would face danger. What kind of danger? He mentions two...

a. *For some, there will be excommunication.*

"They will put you out of the synagogue." We might think, "Well, big deal, if you're forced to leave one synagogue, just find another one." That's a common attitude towards churches today. That's also why we miss the severity of Jesus' warning.

For a Jew to be put out of the synagogue was a hard fate. Jewish life revolved around the synagogue. It was the place of worship. It was the place of teaching. It was also the place of educational opportunity.

Remember, Jesus' disciples were Jews. To be put out of the synagogue was to be ostracized from the community. It affected you financially as well as relationally. If you were put out, you were cut off from your family and cut off from social contacts.

Barclay is right, "Sometimes loneliness among men is the price of fellowship with God." That's what Jesus said would happen to His followers. For some there will be excommunication.

b. *For others, there will be execution.*

John 16:2 again, "A time is coming when anyone who kills you will think he or she is offering a service to God." Jesus' words are solemn, "You will be killed for being My followers, servants. You're going to face terrible persecution."

The book of Acts bears record to this. Stephen was stoned. James beheaded. So goes the record of history.

Countless early Christians were hunted down like animals. Foxe's *Book of Martyrs*, by the way, every Christian needs a copy of this book for your library just to have an account of how those that served their Savior of the stories of believers who were burned at the stake, whose knee-caps were smashed, whose children were drowned, whose joints were systematically and excruciatingly dislocated, why? Because they were bad people? No. It was simply because they belonged to Christ. You say, "The hatred doesn't make sense!" No, hatred never make sense. Yet to this day the martyrdom continues. In the past century, five missionaries were murdered by the Aucas in Ecuador, and who knows how many Christians were imprisoned and executed in the former Soviet Union. I think of men like Dietrich Bonhoeffer the great preacher in Germany that challenged Hitler, and how he died at the hands the Nazis.

And we little know about countless numbers who died in China under Mao's purges (conservative estimates are 12 million), some because they were Christians. Back in the 80's, an average of three pastors a week were being put to death in Ethiopia.

CHAPTER TEN

Do you know what is even more shocking than this? Some of the most severe persecutions in history past have come in the name of God by religious people and by men who thought they were doing the will of God.

That's exactly what Jesus predicted. "Whosoever killeth you will think that he doeth God service" (KJV). The word "service" is the same word used of acts of genuine worship and service in the Bible (see Romans 12:1).

Think of zealous Saul of Tarsus. Prior to his conversion, he hunted down Christians, convinced he was pleasing God. Think of the Crusades. People were killed by sincere zealots, in the name of religion. In the Spanish Inquisition, men thought they were serving God when they tortured heretics into accepting what they considered to be the true faith. As they saw it, they were saving men from hell. And this is hard to fathom, yet true. When Archbishop Cranmer was burned, his executioners actually preached a sermon while he died! You may wonder, "How could a person be so deluded to think that he is doing God a favor by eliminating Christians? It doesn't make sense, does it?" No, that's what Jesus explains next, in John 16:3.

c. *We are dealing with darkness.*

"They will do such things because they have not known the Father or me."

"The world hates you," Jesus said back in John chapter 15. But the world is not just the secular, but includes the religious. You see, biblical Christianity is offensive to those who have mere religion, including those who possess cultural Christianity. Ponder this observation by D. A. Carson, "Nowhere is the world's hatred more clearly set forth than in many people who judge themselves to be 'liberal' but who are most illiberal when it comes to Christian absolutes. They demonstrate their forbearance and large-hearted goodness when they confront diverse options, varied lifestyles and even idiotic practices. But if some Christian claims that Christianity is exclusive (as Jesus insisted), or that moral absolutes exist because they are grounded in the character of God (as the Bible teaches), or that there is a hell to be shunned as well as a heaven to be gained, the most intemperate language is used to excoriate the poor fool. The world hates. "And here's why. We are dealing with *darkness*. What did Jesus say is the reason the world hates? What motivates people to try to get rid of biblical Christianity? John 16:3, "They will do such things because they have not known the Father or me." According to John 16:3, who is in the dark? If one of the following two factors is true, a person is in the dark.

➤ *A person is in the dark if he doesn't know the Father.*

➤ *A person is in the dark if he doesn't know Jesus.*

These two go hand in hand. If you want to know the Father you must know His Son, Jesus. "I am the way, the truth, and the life; no one comes to the Father except by me." Who said that? Jesus did (John 14:6).

It doesn't make sense that the world hates Christianity. It's illogical. But Jesus predicted it would be so, 2000 years ago. He talked frankly to His first followers about these three things: Duty, Danger, and Darkness. He put up a WARNING sign. Why? So they wouldn't be surprised.

CHAPTER TEN

Jesus' warning serves a second purpose. First, His words protect us from doing the wrong thing.

3. Jesus' words prompt us to do the right thing.

Have you heard the story about the pastor who was preaching about heaven? He warned his people that death was coming, and asked the members of his congregation to stand if they could answer yes to one of two questions: "Are you going to heaven? And, if you don't know for sure, do you want to go to heaven?" One little boy remained seated. The pastor singled him out and said, "Son, do you mean you don't want to go to heaven when you die?" The boy replied, "Sure, when I die. I thought you were getting a bunch together to go today."

The boy was obviously confused about the pastor's instructions. Jesus doesn't want us to be confused, so He made it very clear.

When it comes to living in enemy territory, here's the wrong thing to do—"I have told you this so you *will not go astray*." Here's the right thing to do—"I have told you this so that when the time comes *you will remember*."

What must we remember? Two things...

a. We must remember what Jesus said.

"I have told you this, so that when the time comes..."

Notice Jesus said "when" not "if." Hostility is inevitable. And what did Jesus want His disciples to do when they were ridiculed, excommunicated, and even killed? REMEMBER. "When the time comes you will remember that I warned you."

GIVE ME AN OLD SHOE

"What good does remembering do?"

➢ *It will not make the problem go away.* Remember, it's *when* not *if*.

➢ *It does give us security.* How? When we feel the world's hatred, it can actually strengthen our faith in Jesus. It gives us the opportunity to remember, "This is exactly what Jesus predicted would happen and He knows what's happening in my life!"

There's something else we need to remember, first what Jesus *said*, then…

b. We must remember what Jesus did.

In John 16:4 again, "I have told, that when the time shall come, ye may remember that I told you of them. And these things I said not unto you at the beginning, because I was with you."

Let me encourage you to keep this in mind. Jesus didn't give this warning to scare us off.

When as a teen, playing football and baseball, the coach would many times tell us the strengths of the opposition not to put fear in us, but to realize the game would be hard, but if we did what we were taught, told, then we were prepared for what was ahead. Likewise, Jesus warns us, first, so we won't be surprised and go astray. And second, so we will be secure and *remember*.

What Jesus had just announced was new information to His disciples. So up to this point, He had already told them they would be persecuted (Matthew 5:11-12), but until now He had not spelled out the details, so He waited until the night before His crucifixion to tell them. Why not earlier? Why had He waited? Here's the answer He

CHAPTER TEN

gave in verse four, "I did not tell you this at first because I was with you." There's why He waited. As long as He was with them, the venom of the enemy was directed at Him, not them. He shielded them. But that was about to change. Now, as He says in John 15:5, He was leaving.

If we're going to do the right thing while living in enemy territory, we must remember not only what Jesus *said*, but also what He *did*. What did He do? We're told three things right here.

> ➤ *He was once here.* "I was with you," He said. But He couldn't remain on earth forever, not the first time He came. He came to do a work. What work?

> ➤ *He left by way of the cross.* You see, the work Jesus came to do was to save a people by giving His life as a ransom payment for their sins. He did for you what you cannot do, live a perfect life, and when He died on the cross He took upon Himself the penalty you and I deserve to pay for our sins and three days later He rose again.

> ➤ *He is coming again.* For Jesus the suffering was temporary. So for His people He said "A little while, and ye shall not see me: and again, a little while, and ye shall see me," He said in John 16:16 and in verse 22, "And ye now therefore have sorrow: but I will see you again, and your heart shall rejoice, and your joy no man taketh from you." Make It Personal: There is cost involved in true servanthood.

       To follow Jesus is to travel the way of the cross to become the servant and not the served, yes, the blessings are great and the rewards are eternal. Yet the danger is inevitable. As clear as the Bible is on the fact that it cost you nothing to be saved, for Jesus paid the full price, but **IF** you want to be a servant, it will cost you **EVERYTHING** to live for Him and serve Him in enemy territory.

As we conclude this chapter we have found that Jesus knew how to deal with men. In effect, Jesus was saying, "I am offering you the hardest task in the world. I am offering something which will lacerate your body and tear your heart out."

Well, are you **WILLING TO ACCEPT THE OFFER**?

Jesus offered, and still offers, not the way of ease, but the way of glory. Christ still wants men and women who are prepared with open eyes to venture and become the servant for His name.

If we're going to do the right thing while living in enemy territory, we must remember not only what Jesus _said_, but also what He _did_.

CHAPTER TEN

ଔ **11** ଈ

~ *Servanthood* ~
"THY WILL LORD"

T*here* is only one verse that fits this title and it is found in Matthew 6:10 where it reads, "Thy will be done in earth, as it is in heaven."

We know this prayer as "The Lord's Prayer." Maybe it could be more properly called, "The Model Prayer," "The Disciples' Prayer" or "The Pattern Prayer."

Jesus was asked by one, "Lord teach us to pray as John also taught his disciples." It was here that Jesus gave this prayer. It was Dr. George W. Truett that said, "Who on earth knows how to pray this prayer like it ought to be prayed?"

The problem with most of us is that we "run" over it in memory and not pray this prayer from memory without much thought or reverence at all.

Again Dr. Truett said, "Who can scale the heights and sound the depths of that model prayer?" As I listen to Jesus when He said those words, it teaches me that there is one sentence in the prayer that indicates the most important prayer for

CHAPTER ELEVEN

us that are born again, and that is, "Thy will be done." Certainly this should be the prayer of every servant/leader. There is no greater privilege for the Christian on earth than to do the will of God. There is nothing more important than this, nothing! Life teaches us that there is one discordant voice to be heard in this world and that voice is men. Why? Selfishness! It all goes back to the Garden of Eden when man chose to say no to God and it is by his choice and preference.

So as I close out this last chapter, it is important to know that "The Secret of Servanthood" is letting God's will be done in each of our lives so then I want to discuss the meaning of this great prayer.

The highest privilege of human life is to do the will of God. There is no other duty than this – to do the will of God. God has a will and man also has a will and it is the will of God to rule over us. Think about this for a moment, all nature except human nature, obeys the will of God. Man disobeys the will of God; remember Adam and then Eve, when God said not to eat of the tree of knowledge of good and evil, Genesis 2:17? We have to remember that evil is here because of man's will, by his choice. Since man said, "no" in the beginning to God's will, evil is here by man's preference.

What has this got to do with becoming a "servant?" Simply put, that God may have His way with the Christian in this world just as He does with the heavenly host.

Now when you study this prayer, you will find the order. To many times, we reverse this order and ask for "the bread" first, and then God's will to be done. Maybe you are thinking, "Should we not pray for our daily bread?" Sure! Should we not ask about our daily walk in the business world and health, our burdens and daily work? Certainly! It is more important that all of this is for God's kingdom to come on earth.

GIVE ME AN OLD SHOE

What a challenge this prayer is for us. Wherever it takes us, whatever it is or costs, "God's will be done." Believe me it is a challenge, and the most difficult challenge that you and I will ever face in this life.

To pray this prayer without having any reservation is a real test for the believer. To be honest with the reader, I had a hard time praying this prayer as a young Christian. I wanted to be a professional baseball player, and I knew that if prayed that prayer, it would cost me what I wasn't willing to give up. Many years went by before I finally surrendered to that prayer, as I shared in my book, ***"Total Surrender."***

To win this victory over the devil and pray, "thy will be done," there are a couple of thoughts here. First, whose will is it we want done? Well the Bible says, "God's." It is not your will, family will, church will nor your best friend. It is God's will who keeps us, gives us victory in our lives, who crowns us with goodness and marvelous grace. Why should we ever be afraid to serve Him?

A great pastor once said, "His will is the will of love." I know it is hard to understand what I am about to say, but the love of God is tenderer and more loving that the best mother on this earth.

Now secondly, God's will is always best for us, no matter what it is. Back then in my life when it seemed that all was going away from my dream, I could not see the future that my God had for me and my family and certainly I could not see myself becoming a preacher, pastor and servant of people of God. My problem like many, I wanted to be served. After talking with my pastor, he helped me to understand that God's will was best because He deals with us from mercy, grace and love and that His will is always best. There is no greater joy than to serve others!

CHAPTER ELEVEN

"His will is the will of love."

I realized that when we walk by faith, we walk when we can't see the next step ahead of us, then we walk by trust. It was when, I almost lost my wife in an automobile accident, when our baby girl was struck and killed by a car and our home was almost demolished by fire, only four months later, God's will be done! This is why as a servant we must in all areas of our Christian walk, walk by faith, finding out what God's will is for our lives and then take action!

Thirdly, we must realize that this prayer is a call for cooperation with God. What a call from God, to walk with Him and serve with Him! What more can a Christian do for our God here on this earth than to serve others?

There is a wonderful story that I read where some neighbors met to pray for their neighbor, a widow whose husband had left her with a house full of children and with very little to eat and with very little to wear. This group of big, brawny men met one Sunday afternoon to pray that conditions might be better for that poor widow and her family. Right in the middle of their prayers, a big, half-grown boy came in (the son of one of the fathers that did not come) and he put down a great sack of groceries and said, "Pa couldn't come, but he sent his prayers." That's what we are to do. It is time for the church to fortify our prayers with service. Let us undergird the appeal of a lost world and Christians that need to be served, and let us answer our prayers to the last limit of our power and then watch God do the rest!

GIVE ME AN OLD SHOE

Talk about living the victorious Christian life! Paul said it this way, "For to me to live is Christ." Are you living the victorious life? You can.

Fourthly, "as it is in Heaven." How? Well, we know the Bible gives us little glimpses. But just think in heaven there will be no complaining, no grouches and there will be no idlers in that wonderful place.

The next time you are asked to pray about serving in your church, just think of all the blessings that will be yours in Heaven and ask your Lord to help you to do all the good you can, in all the ways you can to all the people you can, until the day God calls you home or when He comes for His church. His will be done, and out of it all, may He bring to pass that which will be best for us and for the glory of His name. And He will, if we relate ourselves joyfully and trustfully to Him.

How can His will be done? It is done wholeheartedly. Heaven is and will be a busy place. A great preacher once said of this, "Some think they will rest there and they will." Dear Christian, there will be no sense of weariness in our Home in Heaven. Just think of the activities which will be ours when we get to Heaven! As His servants we shall serve Him wholeheartedly. There will be no careless, half-hearted service there. Many times here on earth our service is limited, is grudging and coerced. How sad it is today when many Christians give time, talents, and money grudgingly! There will be none of this in Glory.

So, as you complete this chapter and the book, pray this prayer and make it personal. Don't be afraid to pray it. Pray it morning, noon, evening and at night. "Thy will be done." Begin with yourself, wherever it leads. "Thy will Oh Lord......."

CHAPTER ELEVEN

There are two centers—self and Christ. Which one will it be for you? The selfish life is marked inevitably for defeat. The Christ-centered life is marked inevitably for triumph. One has said, "He always wins who sides with Christ; to Him no cause is lost." Dear Christian, side with Christ. Be that servant that God is calling you to be.

GIVE ME AN OLD SHOE

Maybe you have never given your life to Christ, don't hesitate, and decide for Christ now.

Write your decision below:

_____
_____
_____
_____

Date: _____.

SERMONS AND BOOKS

For more information on the following books and sermon series:

Books: ***TOTAL SURRENDER-WALKING BY FAITH***
THE SCARLET THREAD OF REDEMPTION

Series of Sermons:
- **a)** Today's Events-Prophecy and the End Time
- **b)** Questions you have always wanted to ask but..
- **c)** Rejoicing in Revelation
- **d)** The Christians Highest Calling—Worship
- **e)** Great Doctrinal Stones of the Faith
- **f)** Born to Win and Not to Lose

These are available by calling:
Gene Schuyler at 1-919-552-6023

Or write to:
Gene Schuyler
Rebecca Publishing Company
P.O. Box 1521
Fuquay-Varina, NC 27526

www.ingramcontent.com/pod-product-compliance
Lightning Source LLC
LaVergne TN
LVHW091300080426
835510LV00007B/334